101
SUPPORT
GROUP
ACTIVITIES

for
Teenagers
Recovering
from
Chemical
Dependence

Martin Fleming

HAZELDEN

JOHNSON INSTITUTE

Hazelden
Center City, Minnesota 55012-0176
1-800-328-9000 (Toll Free U.S., Canada, and the Virgin Islands)
1-651-213-4000 (Outside the U.S. and Canada)
1-651-213-4590 (24-hour Fax)
www.hazelden.org

Library of Congress Cataloging-in-Publication Data

Fleming, Martin.
    101 support group activities for teenagers recovering from chemical dependence: a leader's manual for secondary educators and other professionals / Martin Fleming.
    p. cm.
    Includes bibliographical references.
    ISBN 1-56246-041-2
    1. Teenagers–Alcohol use. 2. Teenagers–Drug use. 3. Alcoholics–Rehabilitation. 4. Narcotic addicts–Rehabilitation. 5. Group relations training. 6. Self-help groups–Activity programs. 7. Counseling in secondary education. I. Title. II. Title: One hundred one support group activities for teenagers recovering from chemical dependence. III. Title: One hundred and one support group activities for teenagers recovering from chemical dependence.
HV5135.F54 1992   92-15221
362.29'154'0835–dc20   CIP

PRINTED IN THE UNITED STATES OF AMERICA
00 01 02 03 / 5 4 3 2

Cover and text design: Typecetera, Inc.
Illustrations: Harry Pulver, Jr.

Dedication

To all those humble souls who show up early each week to get the coffee going.

Acknowledgments

First off, I'd like to express my heartfelt gratitude to two people who've worked with me on this project from the very start: Lenore Franzen, my editor and guide through the language labyrinth, and Gail Devery, who patiently turned messy manuscript into printed page. I'd also like to thank three support group leaders for the activities they shared with me: Shelley Hansen, Jenni Spear, and Marilyn North.

Table of Contents

Introduction

This book is a collection of activities I've accumulated over the years from leading support groups for young people recovering from chemical dependence. The activities are designed primarily for students in grades 7 though 12 who've had a problem with chemicals and now need help staying clean and sober. Some activities are well-worn favorites I've used in hundreds of support groups; others are designed for special occasions or unusual situations. Regardless, all the activities are structured with two main goals in mind: helping these young people maintain abstinence from mind-altering chemicals and to give them the tools they need to build a healthy and long-lasting program of recovery.

GETTING THEM SOBER IS JUST THE BEGINNING

Julie started drinking at the age of 12. By the time she was 14, it was apparent to everyone that she had some kind of problem. Shortly after her sixteenth birthday, she was diagnosed chemically dependent and admitted to the local chemical dependence treatment center. Now, after 28 days of intensive group and family therapy and twelve-step work, she's returning home with good intentions of not ever again drinking or getting high.

Many recovering teenagers think that when they stop using alcohol or other drugs, all their problems will go away. This illusion fades as soon as they return to school from their treatment experience. When their friends—who are still using chemicals heavily and most likely should also be in treatment—offer them that first joint, they have arrived at a dramatic fork in the road: One way leads to sobriety, maturity, emotional health, and peace of mind; the other leads to despair, family discord, and continued involvement with juvenile court and treatment centers.

With alternatives like that, you'd think the choice would be clear. But it's not. Saying no to that joint means the loss of many things that up to now have been of utmost importance to a chemically dependent teenager. She'll be rejected by her peer group (seen as a "narc," uncool, or plain weird) during a phase in life when friends are everything. She'll be forced to redefine her identity (I used to be a burnout and a partier—who am I now?). And she'll have to turn her back on the one thing that consistently eased the pain, cured her boredom, and helped her cope with stress: getting high and drunk.

The other road, definitely the lesser traveled of the two, is an unknown. In her short sobriety, people have told her that life will be much better for her clean and sober, and she's felt brief moments of happiness and hope, but all of this seems so tenuous, and she wonders if these feelings will last. Alcohol and other drugs have been so predictable, consistent, and easy.

The decision whether to stay clean and sober or to fall back into drinking and getting high is one that recovering young people must make over and over again because whenever they experience uncomfortable feelings the chemicals once again look attractive. And these students have a lion's share of uncomfortable feelings. Besides peer pressure, when recovering young people return to school they face a nightmare of failed classes, incomplete work, and educators skeptical about whether their recently recovering student will be able to turn over a new leaf.

School isn't the only place where there's tension. Home also presents problems. It's common to hear a recovering young person remark, "I've been sober for two months now and my parents *still* don't trust me!" He forgets that his parents have dealt with his crazy behavior, dishonesty, and mood swings for years. And his parents now demand him to be perfect, seeing the smallest infraction as a sign that he must have started getting high once again. Other recovering teenagers are forced to cope with a parent who is still actively chemically dependent, a family situation that offers little or no support.

THE ROLE OF A SUPPORT GROUP

Support groups provide a safe haven for students struggling to stay clean and sober. Here they can find friends who also are recovering from chemical dependence. These peers become their support system at school: in the hall, lunchroom, and parking lot where they're put in contact with former friends who are still using chemicals.

These groups also offer a regular time each week to talk about their feelings, struggles, and fears. Whether having a difficult time at home, struggling with urges to go get wasted, or feeling depressed, the group becomes a healthy, positive resource these young people can turn to. Over time, these peers become a strong unbroken circle, offering support, insight, friendship, laughter.

The group also can be a forum for new ideas, and tips and tools on how to stay clean and sober. Group leaders can introduce topics such as relapse prevention, managing stress, or finding a good twelve-step group. In this way the group not only offers support but continues the learning process begun while in treatment.

A TOOL FOR SUPPORT GROUP LEADERS

This book is primarily a tool for experienced support group leaders who are looking for new and better ways of offering support for young people recovering from chemical dependence. Though it is written with schools in mind, the activities can be readily adapted to a variety of settings: aftercare programs, therapy sessions, treatment centers, youth groups. If you are a beginning support group leader and have more questions than answers at this point, I suggest you read my book *Conducting Support Groups for Students Affected by Chemical Dependence*. This is the basic text for learning how to lead support groups and how to integrate them into your school. Being a support group leader can be a challenge and it requires some training and background in chemical dependence. This book of activities won't teach you how to run a support group—it assumes you already know. Think of this as a cookbook. It doesn't teach you how to cook, but it provides a wealth of new recipes to try.

HOW TO USE THIS BOOK

While many different types of support groups, such as a group for children of alcoholics, adhere to a specific format or curriculum, a group for recovering students should be more flexible. Often, students come to group with problems they need to talk about. This should be the group's first priority. Indeed, answers to the question

"How has your week been?" will often use up the allotted group time. There will be many occasions, though, when group members don't have anything that they wish to discuss. This is a good time to introduce an activity from this book. It's helpful to choose an activity in advance so you'll be prepared.

In addition, as a group leader, you'll become aware of issues that group members struggle with repeatedly, such as relapse, responsibilities, family problems, and relationship issues, among others. When the group is "stuck" on an issue or is misinformed, choose an activity from this book that addresses their particular struggle, and present it the following group session.

The activities in this book are divided into nine categories:

Group development activities help a collection of nervous and uncomfortable students become a cohesive and productive group.

Self-exploration activities help group members understand who they are, what they want, and what they need to change.

Family relations activities help group members understand the emotional dynamics in their family and what they can do to make things better for themselves.

Preventing a relapse activities help group members understand the dynamics of relapse and what they can do to prevent themselves from taking that first drink or joint.

Support systems activities introduce group members to community resources they can turn to for additional help and support.

Goals and decisions activities provide motivation and tools for action based on the insights students gained in the group.

Coping with stress activities teach group members how to recognize and manage their stress.

Coping with peer pressure activities help group members learn how to deal with peer pressure in constructive ways.

Group challenge activities empower group members to work together as a team.

The techniques for teaching these concepts are as varied as the activities. Some activities are discussion-based while others incorporate a game. Since many students can express themselves readily through art, many activities challenge students to draw their thoughts and feelings. And there are also some activities that use physical motion and noncompetitive games as an avenue for personal growth.

Though the heart of this book is the collection of activities, chapter 1 provides a brief description of a support group in action and the final section lists additional resources.

Each activity is organized in the same way. Goals are outlined first, followed by a brief description of the activity. This will help when you're looking for a particular kind of group activity and don't want to have to read several pages just to find out what the activity entails.

Once you've found an activity you're interested in using, the second half of the page provides detailed directions, and a materials list (it's assumed that students will have a pencil or pen and that there is a blackboard or marker board in the room). Worksheets (which have the Look! icon on them) are included for you to photocopy and distribute in group; artwork examples are also included when necessary for clarification. When specific information is required for an activity, there is a **For Your Information** section included so you won't have to hunt down additional resources to present the activity.

Except where noted, all the activities are designed to fit within the time constraints of a typical school class period of about 50 minutes.

THE RATINGS BOX

You might have already noticed that accompanying each activity is a selection code heading with the categories Stage and Challenge.

Stage refers to the developmental stage for which the specific activity is appropriate. The coding system uses the numbers 1 through 4. The first stage is one of building trust and getting acquainted. Group members need to become comfortable with each other and understand how their group will function concerning rules, goals, and expectations.

In stage 2, the newness is over and now group members begin working together. There will be conflict, struggles to define roles, as well as testing of limits and your authority. It's like buying a car: First you look it over; then you kick the tires and take it for a spin.

Once the group has moved through stage 2, then it can get on with the real work of a support group. In stage 3, group members are comfortable and trusting of each other. It's in this setting that students can really take risks and talk about what's going on in their lives.

And since all support group must come to an end, stage 4 describes the process of closure that a group experiences. This should involve more than simply saying good-bye. Stage 4 is a time for students to reflect on what they've learned and experienced as well as to clarify what they will do differently in the future.

Challenge describes the degree of intimacy, honesty, or confrontation the activity requires. Activities designated as low challenge are ideal for beginning groups. Moderately challenging activities will help a support group begin to take the risks necessary to achieve intimacy. Activities with a high level of challenge are often saved for a group that has spent considerable time together. This isn't always the case, though. Sometimes support group leaders, because they have only a few weeks available for the group to meet or because they want to get right to the heart of the matter, will use a high-challenge activity in the beginning stages of the group. **My Story** (activity # 47) is an example of a high-challenge activity you may wish to use as early as the second session because of the intimacy it helps create.

When you refer to the selection code, bear in mind that these are only guidelines for choosing activities for your support group. An activity listed as being appropriate for older students might work very well with a group of younger but mature students, and a stage 3 activity could be modified for use with a fairly new support group.

Above all, as you use these new activities in group, remember that they are simply a medium, a tool, for teaching a concept or creating an opportunity for personal growth. What's really important is our young people and their struggles with the effects of chemical dependence. But even so, we can't just wave a magic wand or simply tell them not to worry. We must point them down the right path, assisting them in developing their own ideas and insights. So, in this light, the tools *are* important. A house to keep you safe and warm might be the goal, but it must be made step by step. And these activities are the tools you can use to help students take those steps from despair to hope, from insight to action that has true recovery as its reward.

Chapter One:
For the Beginning Support
Group Leader

Let's look in the window of a support group for recovering students in progress. Students are sitting in a tight circle of comfortable chairs, talking about things important and personal. The coleaders are sitting across from each other, guiding the process as well as participating in the discussion when appropriate.

The session starts out with a brief warm-up activity to help students focus on their feelings. This is followed by going around the circle once again so all can report to the group whether or not they stayed clean and sober during the previous week, and whether or not they need time during the group session to discuss something personal. Since nobody requests any group time today, the leader introduces the session topic, romantic relationships and recovery.

The coleaders chose this topic in advance because of their concerns resulting from watching group members letting their recovery programs take a backseat to romantic relationships. They ask the group to list both helpful and harmful aspects of relationships regarding the effects on their sobriety.

Sammy points out that the last time a boyfriend dropped her, she went out and got ripped. Tom, currently in a serious relationship, points out that his girlfriend helps him stay sober.

"Huh. So that's why you're always with her and we never see you at any meetings!" snorts Tony, getting a laugh from the rest of the group.

"I go to as many meetings as I need to," Tom says defensively.

"Tony, what are you really trying to tell Tom?" asks one of the leaders.

"Well, that I'm concerned about him . . ."

The leader interrupts, "Don't tell me; tell Tom."

Tony turns in his chair to look straight at Tom. "Tom, I get scared for you, man, when you skip meetings because I know how bad it would be for you if you started doing coke again."

"Does anybody else have any thoughts about Tom's recovery program?" asks the other group leader.

One by one, group members speak up, the majority expressing concern about Tom's lapse in meeting attendance.

"So, how does all this expressed concern make you feel, Tom?" asks the first group leader.

"Well, I think that I can handle it."

"But, that's not what I asked. How are you *feeling* after hearing all this concern about your meeting attendance?"

"Well, defensive, I guess."

"We're only saying it 'cause we care about you, Tom, and don't want you to relapse," says Belinda from across the circle.

"Yeah, I know." After several moments of silence, the other group leader speaks up. "So what are you willing to do about all of this, Tom?"

Tom stares at the floor for a while before answering. "Well, I know I should be going to my Thursday night meeting every week. I promise I'll go every week from now on."

The leader turns to the rest of the group. "Are you happy with that?"

Most of them nod their heads, but Tony speaks up: "And don't blow off your friends to be with Angelene."

Of course, this is merely an example. Support groups change from week to week. And support group leaders have differing styles of running group too. Controlling or loose, intellectual or with their hearts on their sleeves, confrontive or laid back, the flavor of the group depends on the personality of the leaders as well as the students in the group.

We can control some variables of the group experience, such as the physical qualities of the group room, the number of students in group, and the frequency of the group meetings. Every support group leader must make these decisions based on his or her own particular situation. Fortunately, collective experience has brought us practical solutions. Here are some typical questions asked by beginning support group leaders and the answers that work in most situations:

HOW MANY STUDENTS SHOULD I HAVE IN MY GROUP?

The maximum number is much more critical than the minimum number. Six to eight students is a good size; ten should be your upper limit.

IS IT OKAY TO MIX STUDENTS IN MY GROUP?

Most schools only have a handful of students who are recovering; typically, the only option is to work with them together in a single group.

HOW OFTEN SHOULD MY SUPPORT GROUP MEET?

Typically, groups meet once a week, though some recovery groups meet daily, similar to a regular class, and are given assignments and academic credit.

SHOULD GROUPS MEET DURING THE SAME PERIOD EACH SESSION?

While meeting the same period has its advantages—easy for the students to remember, easy for the leaders to prepare—it means that students miss the same class week after week. The best solution is to rotate the group time each week: second period one week, third period next week, and so on.

HOW MANY SESSIONS SHOULD THERE BE?

Recovery groups typically meet for the entire school year, with new members joining the group as they return from a treatment center or express a desire to become part of the group.

SHOULD MY GROUP MEET DURING OR AFTER SCHOOL?

Recovery groups should take place during school and be viewed as an integral part of the school day.

WHERE IS A GOOD PLACE TO HOLD GROUP?

The ideal group room is small, carpeted, and equipped with comfortable chairs. It's also nice to have pillows for when the group is on the floor. There shouldn't be any windows, and the room should be located in a quiet, low-traffic area. Of course, this is the ideal room, and many group leaders must settle for less. Whatever the room, it's important that it be the same room each session of group. Your last choice should be a standard classroom because of the hard floor, large size, chairs with built-in desks, and impersonal atmosphere.

WHAT SHOULD I CALL MY GROUP?

Recovery Group, Relapse Prevention Group, or Sobriety Group are common names. Don't call the group an aftercare group, because that type of group is typically an extension of a student's treatment program and involves group or individual therapy, whereas a support group offers support for sobriety and focuses on school-related issues.

WHAT RULES SHOULD I MAKE FOR MY GROUP?

The fewer the better. Typically rules cover confidentiality, chemical use or possession (No chemicals in you or on you!), regular attendance, and honesty about their sobriety. "Everybody must talk about their feelings" is a hope or expectation—don't make it a rule. And don't make rules that you aren't going to enforce consistently. Students get enough of this inconsistency at home. Keep your rules specific, reasonable, and enforceable.

SHOULD I HAVE ANY ELIGIBILITY REQUIREMENTS TO BE IN THE GROUP?

The group should be open to anyone who has had a problem with chemicals and now is staying—or trying to stay—clean and sober. The majority of group members will have completed a treatment program, but the group should also welcome students who quit using chemicals through other means, such as individual therapy or twelve-step programs. The support group should not include students who never had a problem with chemicals but express a need for support so that they don't start. This student may need support, but from a different group. These two populations are very different and you would have a difficult time getting the students to work together as a group. And, of course, the group shouldn't be open to students who aren't willing to stay clean and sober.

SHOULD I HAVE A COLEADER IN MY GROUP?

In a word, yes. Sometimes conditions make it necessary to run group solo, but whenever possible have a helper. Coleaders can come to the rescue when the group gets unmanageable or when you're not picking up on something that a student is feeling. Beginning group leaders should always have the assistance of a seasoned pro.

WHERE DO I DRAW THE LINE WITH GROUP CONFIDENTIALITY?

Generally speaking, anything that a student says in group stays in group. But, in situations of abuse (physical or sexual), harming one's self (suicide) or harming others (assault or homicide), you must report this information. Explain these exceptions to the confidentiality rule during the first session of group.

On the other hand, a student's group-related behavior, such as sporadic group attendance, could be shared in situations where the information will be put to good use, such as a meeting between parents and school, or a core team discussion (the decision-making team of a school's student assistance program).

SHOULD I ASK STUDENTS TO SIGN NO-USE CONTRACTS?

It depends on how the contract is presented and what the consequences are. Often-times when you demand students to sign a no-use contract, the group becomes dishonest. When a member uses chemicals and breaks his contract (which will happen occasionally), he might be dishonest rather than accept the consequences.

You may wish to make the no-use contract optional. This way the group is both challenging students to maintain sobriety and encouraging honesty.

Some students will enter a support group already on a no-use contract with their parents, the courts, and school. Of course, your support group will then be an extension of this preexisting contract.

IS IT ALL RIGHT FOR STUDENTS TO BE PRESSURED TO ATTEND GROUP EVEN THOUGH THEY DON'T WANT TO BE THERE?

Yes, as long as they don't ruin the group experience for those who do want to be there. For example, a probation officer might make it a condition of probation to attend the school's recovery group, helping a student who was riding the fence put more of an effort into staying sober and also exposing him to other recovering peers. On the other hand, a student who has no intentions of staying abstinent and is forced to come to the recovery group not only won't stay sober very long, she'll also have a negative affect on the group experience for everyone else.

WHAT SHOULD HAPPEN WHEN A GROUP MEMBER USES CHEMICALS?

There is no simple answer to this question. It depends on whether or not the group member brought it to the group's attention of his own accord, if this has happened before, and what he intends to do about it.

If a group member tells the group that he relapsed and truly is trying to stay clean and sober, then most likely the group should allow him to remain in the group. However, it's an altogether different story when a group member is defensive and has to be confronted before admitting to using chemicals. In this case it's not clear whether or not he really is intending to staying clean and sober, or merely staying in group to keep out of trouble at home or with his probation officer. In these and other similar situations, it's best to let the group decide what action to take. It's their group and usually they can make a more accurate appraisal of the situation than can the group leaders.

Some recovery groups follow a policy whereby with the first slip (chemical use), the group votes on the consequence. If a group member slips again, she is automatically out of the group for two weeks and must attend four twelve-step meetings during those two weeks. Then she can rejoin the group, provided she stayed abstinent and attended four meetings.

WHAT'S THE NEXT STEP FOR STUDENTS AFTER THEY'VE FINISHED THE GROUP?

Students don't graduate from this group. As long as they attend the school where the recovery group is offered, they should participate.

The above merely touches on some rather complex and thorny issues surrounding support groups. Again, if you are contemplating initiating a support group in your school, you need more information and training. *Conducting Support Groups for Students Affected by Chemical Dependence* will assist you in developing the framework necessary for support groups to function effectively.

The Activities

Section A:
Group Development Activities

The activities in this first section will transform hesitant students sitting nervously in a circle of chairs into a relaxed and productive support group. A tall order? Not really. Actually, you'll find that after getting the young people to come to the initial group session you're already halfway there. Remember, these students want to talk about their problems, lessen their burdens, stay clean and sober, and connect with peers experiencing similar problems.

Even though many of these students have been in groups before, the group they are beginning with you now is a new experience. They'll know some of the students, while others will be strangers; there might be someone in group whom they don't like, and there may be someone sitting in the circle they don't trust.

Though the focus isn't specifically chemical dependence, all of the activities in this first section are important because they build a secure foundation upon which more challenging activities can be presented. Breaking the ice, building themes of commonality, encouraging students to support each other, and providing transitions to and from the "real world" outside of group are all bricks carefully laid for the structure yet to come.

1
Warm-ups

GOALS: ▶
- Provide a transition from a cognitive to an affective learning mode
- Help students focus on group process
- Energize a lethargic group

DESCRIPTION: ▶

Warm-ups are brief activities used during the first few minutes of group to help students focus on their feelings and group process.

DIRECTIONS: ▶

When first introducing this activity, you should select the warm-up question and pose it to the group. After that, appoint a different group member to select and initiate the warm-up question for each subsequent session. Group members may either make up their own question or choose one from the list you provide (see following page). This activity isn't the mainstay of a group session; it's simply a way to become focused on group process—not unlike a runner stretching before a workout. Five minutes is an adequate amount of time for this activity.

QUESTIONS: ▶

In order to place more responsibility on the group, you could ask the student in charge of the warm-up for the current session to assign next session's warm-up to another group member. This process can then continue each session of group.

MATERIALS: ▶

Warm-up Questions list.

Warm-up Questions

- Name a feeling that's easy for you to talk about. Why?

- Name a feeling that's difficult for you to talk about. Why?

- Are you more like your mother or your father? Why?

- Communicate nonverbally how you are feeling.

- When somebody hurts your feelings, what do you do?

- What do you do when you are angry?

- Tell the group one thing that you appreciate about yourself.

- After everyone is sitting in a tight circle, have them turn to their right and massage their neighbor's neck.

- If you were an animal, what type would you be? Why?

- Demonstrate your personality when you were a little child.

- Name one physical quality about you that you like.

- Identify one quality that you have to offer a friend.

- When was the last time you cried? What were the tears about?

- When you really need to talk to somebody, whom do you turn to?

- What is one thing that people don't understand about you?

- When you need alone time, where do you go and what do you do?

2
Cool-downs

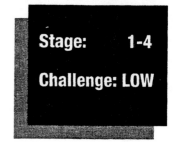

GOALS: ▶
- Provide closure for group activities
- Clarify learning

DESCRIPTION: ▶
Cool-downs are brief activities that bring a raw or unfinished group session to closure and reinforce learning.

DIRECTIONS: ▶
Reserve the last five minutes or so of each group session for this activity. Choose a sentence stem from the following page—appropriate to the activity or discussion the group has just finished—and ask group members to respond.

NOTES: ▶
When a group session hasn't been very intense, you probably won't need a closing activity. You may wish to leave it up to the group to decide. You could also ask group members to choose the closing question.

MATERIALS: ▶
Cool-downs List.

Cool-downs List

- Ask group members what they learned about themselves today.

- Tell a joke.

- Ask everyone to get up and stretch.

- Hold hands and be silent for two minutes.

- Tell the group members something you appreciate about them.

- Ask a member of the group to summarize what happened during the group.

- Ask group members to tell a person in group who is having an especially difficult time something they appreciate about her.

- Ask group members what they need from the rest of the group.

- Ask the group what they would like to do next week.

- Ask group members if they have anything they would like to say to the rest of the group.

3
Group Rituals

GOALS: ▶

■ Create an opening or closing ritual for group sessions
■ Provide consistency and unity within the group

DESCRIPTION: ▶

Students create an opening or closing ritual that can be used in each session of group.

DIRECTIONS: ▶

Going around the circle, ask group members to identify at least two personal rituals they perform regularly, such as falling asleep in the same manner, saying a prayer before eating dinner, or even how they say good-bye to friends. Point out to the group that rituals have value because they provide predictability and meaning to our lives. Therefore, a ritual will be helpful for the group also. Ask the group to think of some rituals that the group could adopt (see following page for a list of possible group rituals). Once the group has chosen a ritual, then it should be performed every time the group meets, without fail.

MATERIALS: ▶

None required.

Group Rituals List

- Repeat the Serenity Prayer

- A group hug

- Stand in a circle and silently hold hands

- Sing a song

- A special handshake

- Report one word describing how you feel today

- Identify something you learned about yourself today in group

- Read a passage out of the Big Book of Alcoholics Anonymous

- Read out of a daily meditation book

- Read the **"I Am" Creed** (see activity 48)

4
Why Am I Here?

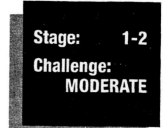

GOALS:

- Encourage self-disclosure
- Create group unity
- Provide a foundation for future group activities

DESCRIPTION:

Group members explain their backgrounds and why they are in the group.

DIRECTIONS:

There are a variety of circumstances that bring students to group. Some have just finished a treatment program, some have been abstinent for a time, and others are just beginning to attempt to quit using alcohol and other drugs. All of this needs to be discussed, for the benefit of group leaders as well as other group members. Besides creating an understanding of the backgrounds and issues present, this activity will help create intimacy in the group.

QUESTIONS:

- What circumstances have brought you to this group?
- Have you gone through a treatment program?
- Why do you want to be in this group?
- How long have you been clean and sober?
- Do you have to be here? What happens if you don't come?

MATERIALS:

None required.

5
Take What You Need

GOALS: ▶
- Encourage self-disclosure
- Reduce communication barriers

DESCRIPTION: ▶ Group members volunteer information about themselves.

DIRECTIONS: ▶ Place a container of M&Ms or a roll of toilet paper in the center of the group circle. Tell group members to take what they need. At this point, don't give any further instructions. After everyone has taken what they want, tell the group that everyone must share one thing about themselves for each M&M or square of toilet paper they've taken. Go around the circle as many times as are required. Group members should be encouraged to share anything they wish.

NOTES: ▶ If you use M&Ms, it would be a good idea to limit the amount you place in the circle. Otherwise some students could grab such a large handful that they would need several hours of sharing time!

MATERIALS: ▶ M&Ms or toilet paper.

6
Five Things We Have In Common

GOALS: ▶
- Establish group rapport
- Encourage honest communication

DESCRIPTION: ▶

Group members break into teams of two or three, and find five things that they all share in common.

DIRECTIONS: ▶

Depending on the number of students in the group, divide the students into teams of two or three. Instruct them to discover something that each member of the team shares in common. This could be age, owning a dog, or liking the same music. After the team has found this commonality, ask them to repeat the task, but this time give them a focus, such as characteristics of parents, things they're afraid of, or feelings they don't like dealing with. Each time you repeat the task, make the specific focus more difficult and personal.

NOTES:

You may wish to shift team members at some point in this activity so students have a chance to get to know other group members.

MATERIALS:

None required.

7
Sentence Stems

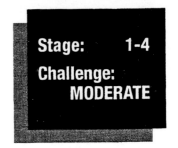

GOALS: ▶
- Encourage honest communication
- Allow students to determine the session's focus

DESCRIPTION: ▶
Group members take turns choosing and completing sentence stems.

DIRECTIONS: ▶
Distribute copies of sentence stems (see following page) and ask each group member to choose and answer a question in turn. After a student answers a question, the rest of the group can ask for more information or clarification. Tell the group they can make up their own questions if they can't find a question on the sheet that they like.

NOTES: ▶
Give everyone a copy of the questions, so time isn't wasted while students read through the list looking for a question to answer. A variation of this activity would be to ask the person who just answered a question to choose the question for the next group member.

MATERIALS: ▶
Sentence Stems List for each group member.

Sentence Stems List

1. Right now I'm feeling . . .
2. When I'm alone I feel . . .
3. When I'm surrounded by people I feel . . .
4. One thing that I hate is . . .
5. One thing that I really like about myself is . . .
6. When I'm feeling sad I . . .
7. The last time I cried was . . .
8. When I daydream it's usually about . . .
9. I'm afraid of . . .
10. I'm the happiest when . . .
11. One thing that really worries me is . . .
12. If I could change one thing about myself it would be . . .
13. If I could be with anyone right now I would be with . . .
14. The family member I'm closest to is . . .
15. If I was really honest with my father I would tell him . . .
16. One thing I regret about my life is . . .
17. If I only had one more day to live I would . . .
18. If I was really honest with my mother I would tell her . . .
19. One thing about me that nobody knows is . . .
20. I hope that someday in the future . . .
21. When I think about my family I feel . . .
22. Something I feel really embarrassed about is . . .
23. One thing about me I never want to change is . . .
24. One thing I feel really proud of is . . .
25. This support group has helped me to . . .
26. One thing I like about all of you is . . .

8
Recovery Rap

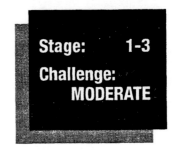

Stage: 1-3
Challenge: MODERATE

GOALS: ▶	■ Expose students to recovery concepts ■ Help students maintain a quality sobriety ■ Provide a forum for open discussion
DESCRIPTION: ▶	Students spend the group session discussing a variety of topics related to recovery.
DIRECTIONS: ▶	Pass around the **Recovery Rap List** (see following page) and ask the group to choose a topic to begin the discussion. Once the topic has been chosen, encourage the group to take responsibility for the ensuing discussion. Don't jump to fill in moments of silence. These young people need to form a cohesive group that works together as a team, and one of their first challenges is to learn how to discuss issues that affect them all. Any one of the topics on the list should be able to generate enough discussion to fill an entire group session. Encourage them to ask each other questions that will expand the discussion, such as, "How did you feel when that happened?" "What happened then?" or "Tell us more about it." You may even wish to appoint an impromptu student group leader who helps other students spend more time answering each question.
NOTES: ▶	You may wish to schedule this activity on, say, the last week of every month to allow the group to practice taking responsibility for working together as a discussion group.
MATERIALS: ▶	**Recovery Rap List**.

Recovery Rap List

1. What was your life like when you were using chemicals?

2. What is involved in your Recovery Program?

3. Describe your family.

4. Why did you decide to quit using alcohol and other drugs?

5. Is it difficult for you to stay sober? Why or why not?

6. Have you ever had a slip? How and why did it happen?

7. Do you go to twelve-step meetings? Why or why not?

8. Do you have a boyfriend or girlfriend now? Does this person use chemicals?

9. Does your family make it easier or harder for you to stay sober?

10. What do your friends think about you quitting using alcohol and other drugs?

11. If you were going to die tomorrow, would you use chemicals today? Why or why not?

12. Does anyone else in your family have a problem with chemicals?

13. Have you been through a treatment program before? What was it like?

14. What helps you stay clean and sober?

15. Now that you're sober, what other personal problems are you working on?

16. Describe your best day since you've quit using chemicals.

17. Why do you think you ended up having a problem with alcohol and other drugs?

18. What's the hardest part about staying clean and sober?

19. What does your family think about you quitting using chemicals?

20. Why are you a member of this support group?

9
Grumpy

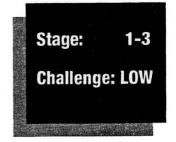

Stage: 1-3

Challenge: LOW

GOALS: ▶
- Provide noncompetitive recreation
- Break up the intensity of other group sessions

DESCRIPTION: ▶ Group members try to make one designated person laugh.

DIRECTIONS: ▶ Explain to the group that this game involves attempting to keep a straight face despite the antics performed by the rest of the group. Ask for a volunteer to be "it" first. She should sit in the center of the circle while the rest of the group tries their best to make her laugh or crack a smile, but without touching her in any way. Group members should take turns trying to evoke a laugh, working around the circle. Whoever is successful in making her laugh gets to be in the center next.

After playing this game for most of the group session, spend some time talking about laughter and its benefits. Ask the group to think about and then discuss situations in which they can let go and laugh.

MATERIALS: ▶ None required.

10
Two Coyotes and a Rabbit

Stage: 1-3

Challenge: LOW

GOALS: ▶
- Provide noncompetitive recreation
- Encourage students to talk about themselves

DESCRIPTION: ▶

Group members play a chase game using three balls and talk about themselves when they are caught.

DIRECTIONS: ▶

Ask group members to stand and form a circle. Throw two basketballs out into the circle and ask group members to begin *passing* them around. These two basketballs are the coyotes and they can only be passed to neighboring group members—not across the circle. Once the group has gotten accustomed to these basketballs moving around the circle, throw out the volleyball. Tell the group that this ball, being the rabbit, can jump across the circle as well as move around the circle. Now all three balls will be moving in the circle. The object of the game is to avoid having the coyotes catch the rabbit, which occurs when a group member is holding the rabbit and is also passed one or both coyotes. If one coyote catches the rabbit, the game stops momentarily and the group member who was holding the rabbit must tell something about himself. If both coyotes catch the rabbit, the game pauses and the rest of the group creates a question for the group member who was holding the rabbit to answer.

NOTES: ▶

If this game is played in the group room, put any breakables, like lamps or vases, away for safekeeping. Playing this game in a gymnasium or other recreation area is preferable because sometimes the playing can get a little wild. Another idea would be to use softer and lighter balls, such as beach balls or foam rubber balls.

MATERIALS: ▶

Two basketballs and one volleyball.

11 Pulse

GOALS: ▶
- Encourage group cooperation
- Provide noncompetitive recreation

DESCRIPTION: ▶ One student stands in the center of the group circle while the remaining students join hands and pass a squeeze around the circle. The student in the center tries to locate this "pulse."

DIRECTIONS: ▶ Ask group members to form a tight circle sitting cross-legged and holding hands. Tell the group that the object of this game is to pass a "pulse" around the circle without getting caught. This pulse is represented by the squeezing of hands. When a group member feels her right hand getting squeezed, for example, she then passes the pulse on by squeezing the group member's hand on her left. In this way the pulse is passed around the circle. The job of the person in the center is to catch the pulse after someone has received it, but before she has gotten rid of it.

Once the group has gotten the hang of passing the pulse, show them how they can reverse the direction of the pulse by squeezing back the same hand that squeezed theirs. This makes it much more difficult, but not impossible, for the person in the center to catch the pulse.

Once everyone is familiar with the game, start by asking someone to be in the center of the circle. Ask a student who is out of view of the person in the center to start the pulse. Once the pulse is moving, the student in the center is free to spin around and try to catch the pulse by pointing to someone and saying this person's name when he thinks she has the pulse. If he's correct, these two switch places and a new round starts; if he isn't correct, the game continues.

MATERIALS: None required.

12
Guess Who I Am

Stage: 2

Challenge: HIGH

GOALS: ▶

- Encourage honest communication
- Identify inaccurate self-perceptions
- Increase self-esteem

DESCRIPTION: ▶

Students write two brief personality sketches—the first concerning how they view themselves, and the second how they think the rest of the group views them. After guessing the correct identity of the sketches, the group discusses the second set of sketches.

DIRECTIONS: ▶

Ask group members to write brief personality sketches about themselves. This short, one- or two-paragraph sketch should describe their mannerisms, how they interact with others, common moods, likes and dislikes, and so on. Once they've finished the first sketch, ask them to write another similar sketch on the bottom half of the paper, but this second sketch should focus on how they think the rest of the support group views them. In short, what do they think other students in the group think about them?

Once everyone has finished writing, collect the sketches and mix them up in a stack. Read the first sketch in the pile out loud to the group and ask them to guess who they think is the author. After everyone has guessed, identify the person who wrote the sketch and then read the second part—how this person thinks the rest of the group sees her—to the group. As you read this second sketch, pause after each specific point and ask the group if they agree or disagree. For example, if a group member wrote, "My support group thinks I am shy and quiet," ask the group if they agree. "Do all of you see Kathy as shy and quiet?"

After reading the entire second sketch, ask the group to make additions to the sketch that the author didn't include—"Well, Kathy didn't say anything about how she always tries to help other people in the group when they are feeling down," for example. Follow this same routine for every group member's set of personality sketches.

MATERIALS:

Paper and pencils.

13
Eavesdropping

GOALS: ▶
- Discover new solutions to students' problems
- Encourage feedback from the group

DESCRIPTION: ▶ One group member sits outside the circle while the remainder of the group discusses his problems and possible solutions within his hearing distance.

DIRECTIONS: ▶ After explaining this activity to the group, ask for a volunteer. Inform the group that everyone will get a turn. Ask the volunteer to take her chair and sit some five feet outside the group circle with her back to the group. Tell her that she can listen to the conversation within the group, but that she can't respond until after they're finished and invite her back to the circle.

Now, with her removed from the circle, ask the rest of the group to discuss this person: her recovery program, the things about her that they appreciate, the things about her that concern them, what they think she should do to improve her situation. When they are finished, ask her to rejoin the circle, allowing her to respond to the group's suggestions if she wishes. Discourage defensive justifications, however, reminding her that this is simply opinions of other group members and she is free (as they say in a number of twelve-step programs) to take what she likes and leave the rest.

Use the rest of the session for other group members to be the focus of attention.

NOTES: ▶ You may wish to place the student being discussed behind a screen. This additional anonymity for the rest of the group encourages them to share their thoughts honestly. At times you may need to steer the conversation back towards a constructive focus if group members make inappropriate comments in an attempt to be humorous.

MATERIALS: ▶ None required.

14
One Thing I Like About You

Stage: 3
Challenge: HIGH

GOALS: ▶
- Encourage the giving and receiving of compliments
- Allow students to take risks in a safe environment
- Increase self-esteem

DESCRIPTION: ▶

Each group member gives a compliment to one group member who is chosen to be the focus of attention. Every student is given the opportunity to receive compliments from the rest of the group.

DIRECTIONS: ▶

Discuss the importance of self-esteem with the group, pointing out that though it's sometimes embarrassing to be given compliments, it sure makes us feel good. And it's important to feel good about ourselves, that we matter, that we have something to offer.

Choose someone to be the center of attention and then proceed around the circle, asking everybody to give a compliment to this particular student. When all have shared something, pick someone else (or ask for volunteers) to be the focus and repeat the sharing until everyone has had a chance to be the center of attention.

After everyone has received compliments, discuss the group members' reactions to being the focus of so many compliments. Encourage them to think about how they typically react to compliments they receive from family and friends.

QUESTIONS: ▶
- How did it feel to be given these compliments?
- Was it harder to give them or to receive them?
- Would it be okay to ask friends or family to give you some compliments when you are feeling down? Why or why not?

NOTES: ▶

This isn't an activity for a group in its beginning stages. In fact, this activity won't even work in some groups that have been meeting for a long time because of the personal risk involved. When this activity does work, though, it's wonderfully effective at providing an avenue for group members to give each other sincere and powerful compliments.

MATERIALS: ▶

None required.

15
Spin the Bottle

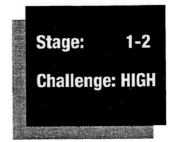

GOALS: ▶
- Create intimacy within the group
- Encourage the sharing of important personal information

DESCRIPTION: ▶

Students play spin the bottle and ask each other questions of their own choosing.

DIRECTIONS: ▶

Have the group sit in a tight circle on the floor and place a pop bottle in the center. Begin the game by spinning the bottle. Whomever the bottle points to gets to go first. She spins the bottle again and whomever it points to now must think of a question to ask the person who spun the bottle. If she doesn't want to answer this question, she may pass and spin the bottle again to be asked a new question by a different group member. Once she answers the question, the person who asked the question gets to spin the bottle to continue the game.

NOTES: ▶

The questions asked during this game often become very personal. As long as the group is okay with the risky nature of the questions, this game will quickly begin to create intimacy within the group. Usually the questions don't get too aggressive because the person who asks the question knows that he will be on the hot seat next. If the questions are becoming (for the group as a whole) uncomfortably bold, you may wish to require that the person asking the question must also answer the same question.

MATERIALS: ▶

Pop bottle.

16
My Secret Pal

GOALS:

- Encourage group unity
- Build self-esteem
- Encourage students to be observant of others
- Provide evaluation of growth and learning

DESCRIPTION:

Students are anonymously assigned to another member of the group. Their task is to observe their secret pal discreetly, and then, after at least several sessions, give their pal his or her observations.

DIRECTIONS:

Write each group member's name on a separate slip of paper and place them in a hat or face down on a table. Ask group members to draw a slip, but not to share the name they draw with anyone else. After drawing names, tell the group that they are to observe their secret pal during future group sessions, looking for positive changes, such as risks taken or feelings being shared. They should do this discreetly, though, so that nobody knows who their secret pal is.

At some point during the last few sessions of the group experience, ask group members to reveal their partner's name and to share what they have observed. A student might have noticed that her partner was shy at first but eventually opened up and started sharing lots of feelings, or a secret pal might have observed that his partner always was helping others and putting everybody at ease.

QUESTIONS:

- What did you notice about your secret pal?
- Did your secret pal suspect you were observing her?
- How has your secret pal changed during the course of this group?

NOTES:

You may wish to make the observation phase of this activity span the entire length of the group experience, because the revelation of secret pal identities and the sharing of observations can be a great closing activity. Regardless of how many sessions you elect to span, it is best not to assign secret pals until the group is comfortable and familiar with each other, perhaps no earlier than the third or fourth session.

MATERIALS:

Slips of paper.

17
Group Inventory Checklist

GOALS: ▶
- Reflect on the health and progress of the group
- Encourage self-inventory
- Promote positive group dynamics

DESCRIPTION: ▶
Students discuss questions on a checklist in order to assess the health of their support group as a whole.

DIRECTIONS: ▶
Explain to the group that just as we individually need to ask ourselves how we are doing from time to time, so does the group as a whole. Give the checklist (see following page) to a member of the group and ask her to choose a question for the group to discuss. If a group discussion doesn't naturally occur, you may ask each group member in turn to answer the specific question before proceeding with the next question. Let everyone have a chance to choose a question for the group to answer.

NOTES: ▶
As the group leader, it's appropriate for you also to answer questions put to the group. It's best to add your comments after everyone else has spoken except for those occasions when the group is hesitant to share their thoughts about a particular question, such as "Are there cliques in our group?"

MATERIALS: ▶
Group Inventory Checklist.

Group Inventory Checklist

1. Does our group help us?

2. Is our group enjoyable?

3. Do we encourage everyone to participate?

4. Does our group feel safe?

5. Does everyone participate in group, or do some members just take up space?

6. Do our group leaders do a good job at helping us?

7. Are there things we should be talking about but don't?

8. Do we spend too much time on some subjects?

9. Is anyone made fun of in group?

10. Are group rules being broken?

11. Are there cliques in our group?

12. Is there something that the group leader isn't doing that should be done?

13. Do people interrupt each other?

14. Do we volunteer information, or do we wait for the group leader to ask us?

15. What is great about our group?

16. How could we improve our group?

18
Sobriety Celebration

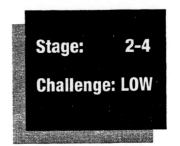

Stage: 2-4

Challenge: LOW

GOALS: ▶
- Give students recognition for their sobriety
- Encourage students to stay sober

DESCRIPTION: ▶ Students have a party honoring group members who are celebrating abstinence birthdays.

DIRECTIONS: ▶ There are many different approaches you may wish to pursue when honoring sobriety birthdays. The main point is to recognize and affirm students for staying clean and sober for a period of time, be it a week, a month, three months, or a year. All of these dates are important and worthy of note.

You may wish to set aside some time during the last group session of each month for celebrating birthdays. By asking the group "Who is celebrating a week of sobriety? A month? Three months?" and so on, everybody will be able to take part in the celebration. And so they should. A single week is just as important to the teenager who did the struggling as is the three months for another group member.

You may wish to make special note of certain time intervals, such as three, six, and nine months. And there should be much hoopla for a year of continuous sobriety. These intervals can be noted by medallions, birthday cakes with candles, special outings. Consider taking the support group out for a pizza lunch when someone celebrates a year of sobriety. During the celebration, ask the birthday girl to make a short speech telling the group what it's been like staying sober, and how the group has helped her through the tough times, for example.

NOTES: ▶ In order to keep track of upcoming sobriety birthdays, you may wish to keep a record of their birthdays so that you can prepare ahead of time. Confirm this birthday with the student, though, before buying the cake. Sometimes these birthdays can change.

MATERIALS: ▶ Medallions, certificates, cakes.

19
Support Group Party

GOALS: ▶
- Celebrate the time spent together in group
- Validate personal work students have accomplished
- Bring about closure to the group

DESCRIPTION: ▶
Group members plan and then have a party during one of the last sessions of group.

DIRECTIONS: ▶
Ask group members to plan a party for the following week of group. This party should take place during one of the last sessions of group, although there might be other times when it also would be appropriate, such as the week before Christmas break. Place most of the responsibility for the party on the group's shoulders. They should decide who will be responsible for bringing music, refreshments, and what will happen during the party, such as playing games or listening to music.

NOTES: ▶
Some groups can't handle unstructured time well. If this is the case in your group, you might ask the group members to plan specific activities for the party.

MATERIALS: ▶
Refreshments, music, games.

Section B:
Self-exploration Activities

Basic communication skills, an understanding of our feelings, and recognition of who we are and what we want are fundamental to recovery from chemical dependence.

Recovering teenagers in your support group used to use a seemingly easy way out—alcohol and other drugs. The chemicals were a salve for many hurts: low self-esteem, poor communication skills, loneliness, family dysfunction, physical or sexual abuse. Most members of your group either lost their self-awareness through extensive chemical use, or they never knew themselves to begin with. Regardless, the activities in this section are designed to bring clarity and a realistic self-picture by helping group members focus on feelings, attitudes, and past experiences. Those group members who graduated from a treatment program have already begun this process. For them, these activities will be opportunities for further work. Most likely, though, there will also be students in your group who haven't been through a treatment program. These young people will be merely beginning to understand what it is that makes them tick and will find these activities especially helpful and relevant.

20
Life Maps

GOALS: ▶

- Validate personal experiences
- Establish group unity
- Familiarize leaders with students' family histories

DESCRIPTION: ▶

Students draw a time line of their lives that illustrates their past experiences with chemical dependence in their family.

DIRECTIONS: ▶

Pass out blank sheets of newsprint paper and markers and give the students an entire group session to draw the chronological history of their lives—from when they were born to the present. They should include anything that's significant to them: moving, parent's divorce, first kiss, changing schools, going to treatment, and so on. Undoubtedly, they will want to know how to record this information, so discuss a few approaches: *linear progression*—construct a time line, placing significant events in chronological order; *boxed captions*—draw squares and sketch different scenes in each; *journal entries*—write the events and the accompanying feelings (see following page for a sample **Life Map**). Encourage students to be creative and make sure they understand the importance of including their own feelings associated with the past events.

Several sessions of group after this activity should be used to share these life maps. Ask two other members of the group to hold the student's life map for the rest of the group to see while he explains the contents. Give all members a reasonable amount of time to discuss their life map with the group. If students are hesitant to share, or if they skip over things, slow them down by asking questions. Typically, group members will want to give only superficial information: "This happened, and then that happened, and then my brother. . ." This isn't what you want. Instead, ask questions that encourage identifying feelings: "How did you feel inside when your brother did that?" "How did you feel when your mom left your dad?" Encourage other group members to ask questions too; this will set the stage for the group to function as a group rather than the leader always asking the questions.

NOTES: ▶

You should cover between two and three life maps each session of group. More than three life maps in one session means you are moving too quickly; instead, ask additional questions and encourage the students to talk in more depth. Less than two means the students are sharing quite a bit, but it also means that you will be dealing with life maps for many weeks to come.

Remember to be gentle when you ask further questions about a group member's life map. This activity is designed to help group members connect feelings with experiences, and to disclose information to their peers, not for them to relive painful episodes.

MATERIALS: ▶

Large sheets of newsprint, markers, or crayons.

LIFE MAP

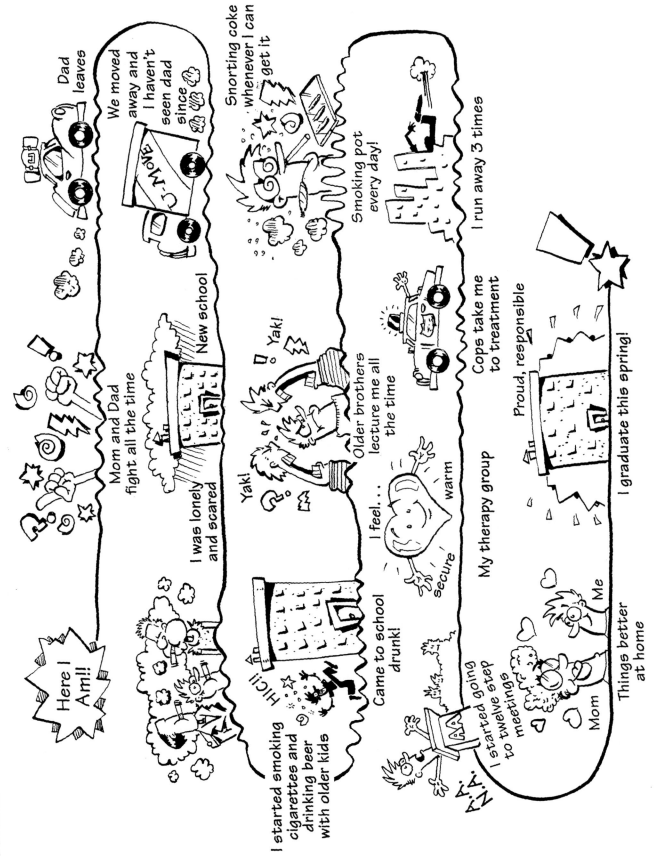

21
My Life Song

GOALS: ▶
- Reflect on personal experiences
- Encourage creativity and self-expression

DESCRIPTION: ▶ Students choose a favorite song and rewrite the lyrics as a poem about themselves.

DIRECTIONS: ▶ Ask group members to each choose a song they like and are familiar with. Then tell them to write their own lyrics to this song using themselves as the theme. They may wish to tell the story about their chemical dependence, describe their personalities, or whatever they wish, as long as it's something about themselves. Give them some time to compose one or two verses to the song, writing the words down on a sheet of paper in poem format. When everyone has done this, ask group members to read the lyrics out loud to the group. Encourage them to sing the lyrics if they are willing. Let them know it doesn't matter if they sing off-key; everyone will recognize the song and be able to follow along.

NOTES: ▶ The group may even wish to compose a group theme song that they can all sing from time to time.

MATERIALS: ▶ Paper.

22
My Two Sides

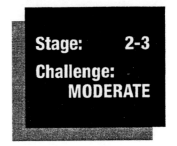

GOALS: ▶

- Identify personal defenses
- Encourage discussion of secret feelings

DESCRIPTION: ▶

Group members explore the differences between their public and private feelings by labeling these feelings on an outline of their body.

DIRECTIONS: ▶

Ask group members to draw a large outline shape of themselves on newsprint. If the newsprint is large enough, they can lie down on the paper and have a friend trace their body on the paper. Inside the figure they should detail the feelings they keep to themselves and outside the figure, the feelings they reveal to the world around them. After everyone has done this, the disparity between the inside and outside should be discussed.

QUESTIONS: ▶

- What feelings do you have hidden inside?
- How do you present yourself to your family? to your friends?
- Why is there a difference between your inside feelings and your outside feelings?
- Why are some feelings harder to share than others?

NOTES: ▶

If you are instructing group members to draw their actual body outlines, be sensitive to possible uncomfortable feelings of a group member who is overweight.

MATERIALS: ▶

Large sheets of newsprint or bulletin board paper and markers.

23
Fantasy Islands

GOALS: ▶
- Clarify personal values
- Identify personally important people and places
- Encourage discussion of present circumstances

DESCRIPTION: ▶
Group members draw their own island country, deciding who and what to include. The islands are discussed when everyone has finished drawing.

DIRECTIONS: ▶
After handing out large sheets of newsprint, tell group members to draw the outline of a large island that will be their own. After they have drawn the island's shape, let them know that, because this is their island, they are in charge of who and what is on the island. And because this is a fantasy island, anything goes: Candy trees, rivers of warm water, a house built out of gold, a remote section of the island for their parents to live, no rules, lots of rules. Encourage them to be creative (see following page for an example). Save some time at the end of the session for group members to discuss their islands.

QUESTIONS: ▶
- Who is welcome on your island?
- What is especially important about your island?
- What aspects of your island are similar to your life now?
- What aspects of your island are different from your life now?
- What does Julie's island tell us about her? (Ask the rest of the group).

NOTES: ▶
If the group seems hesitant or unsure of this task, it's best for you, as the group leader, to just start drawing your own island—soon the others will follow suit.

MATERIALS: ▶
Large sheets of newsprint, markers, and crayons.

FANTASY ISLAND

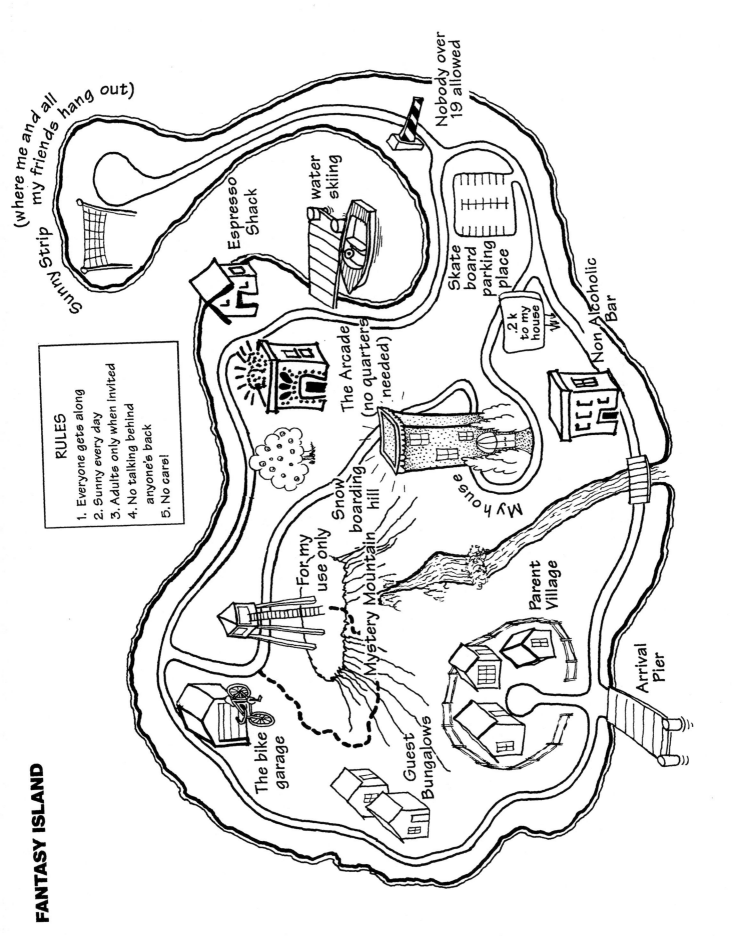

(where me and all my friends hang out)

Sunny Strip

Nobody over 19 allowed

water skiing

Espresso Shack

Skate board parking place

.2 k to my house

Non Alcoholic Bar

RULES
1. Everyone gets along
2. Sunny every day
3. Adults only when invited
4. No talking behind anyone's back
5. No cars!

The Arcade (no quarters needed)

My house

For my use only

Snow boarding hill

Mystery Mountain

Parent Village

The bike garage

Guest Bungalows

Arrival Pier

24
Draw Your School

GOALS: ▶
- Communicate feelings and attitudes about school
- Explore the relationship between school and personal issues

DESCRIPTION: ▶

Group members draw personal impressions of their school, including their classrooms, teachers, and other students.

DIRECTIONS: ▶

Ask group members to close their eyes and imagine their school, classrooms, and the teachers they interact with throughout the day. Ask them to concentrate on their emotional responses to their school day. How does it feel to sit in a boring class? How does it feel to struggle with sobriety while some students use lots of drugs?

After they have an emotional picture of their school experience in mind, hand out large sheets of newsprint and ask them to draw their school and the significant people they interact with there. Point out that their drawings should focus on this emotional picture—they shouldn't try to make their drawings a true physical representation of the school (see following page for an example).

Once everyone has finished, spend the remaining time discussing these drawings.

QUESTIONS: ▶
- What feeling words would you use to describe your school?
- What aspects of school do you like the most? the least?
- Are there adults in the school whom you could talk to if you had a problem? Who are they?
- Is it difficult for you to stay clean and sober at school?
- What can you change to make school a more positive experience for yourself?

MATERIALS: ▶

Newsprint and markers.

MY SCHOOL DRAWING EXAMPLE

25
My Song

GOALS: ▶
- Clarify personal values
- Identify personally important people and places
- Encourage discussion of current issues

DESCRIPTION: ▶
Group members bring lyrics of a favorite song to group and, after reading them out loud, discuss why the lyrics are important to them.

DIRECTIONS: ▶
The week previous to this session, ask group members to choose a favorite song and bring the lyrics to group. Tell them they will be asked to explain the song's personal importance. The following week ask group members to read the lyrics to their songs out loud and then explain to the group why the song is important.

QUESTIONS: ▶
- Why did you choose this song?
- What do you think this song's message is?
- How does this song make you feel?
- Why is this song important to you?

NOTES: ▶
Be aware of the fact that some students might bring lyrics that contain profane language or lyrics promoting sexism, racism, or other offensive actions. If you feel uncomfortable including these topics in group discussion, you may not want to use this activity. Another option would be to say something like "Choose a favorite song that doesn't contain any objectionable language or content."

MATERIALS: ▶
None required.

26
Whole Person Wheel

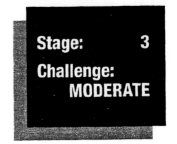

GOALS: ▶

■ Create awareness of personal needs
■ Help students understand their personalities

DESCRIPTION: ▶

Students respond to a number of sentence stems that challenge them to think about who they are and what they need.

DIRECTIONS: ▶

Pass out sheets of newsprint and ask group members to write the word *I* in the center and draw a small circle around it. Then they should draw eight equally spaced lines outward to the edge of the paper from the center, like the spokes of a wheel. Towards the middle, they should write the following words, one in each section: want, am, have, love, hate, fear, wish, and need. Once done, ask group members to spend some time thinking about and then filling in the triangle sections with appropriate endings to the sentence stems. For example, I need . . . people who care about me, love from my family; I wish . . . my Dad would quit drinking, Liz would go out with me. Encourage them to fill in as many examples as they can for each section. Reserve some time at the end of the session to share answers within the group.

MATERIALS: ▶

Sheets of newsprint and markers.

27
Journaling

Stage: 2-4

Challenge: LOW

GOALS:
- Encourage students to reflect on their thoughts and feelings
- Increase self-awareness
- Strengthen writing skills

DESCRIPTION:

Group members are taught how to record their thoughts and feelings in a journal.

DIRECTIONS: ▶

Introduce the concept of journaling to the group by explaining the positive aspects of keeping a journal:

It helps you understand your own thoughts and feelings.

It provides an avenue for expressing thoughts and feelings that you wouldn't ever share with others.

You can read back through previous entries and see how your feelings and problems have changed over time.

Tell the group that each week, the first five minutes of group will be set aside for writing in journals. Make sure the group members understand that they can write whatever they wish, and that nobody will read their journals. They are private. They can keep their journals in the group room or, if they want to write more during the week, they can take the journals with them and bring them back each week.

NOTES: ▶

You may wish to expand on this activity. Here are several different options to consider:

1. After the group has finished writing each week, ask if anybody would like to share what he or she has written.
2. Near the last session of the support group, set aside one session for students to read through their journals and then discuss what has changed during the course of the group sessions as evidenced by their journal entries.

Regardless of how this activity is handled, make sure you show group members that you take their privacy seriously by carefully collecting and putting their journals away in a safe place each week.

MATERIALS:

Spiral notebooks or sheets of lined paper stapled together (one sheet for each session of group).

28
My Sober Future

GOALS: ▶
- Reinforce the importance of continued abstinence
- Encourage students to look positively towards the future

DESCRIPTION: ▶

Students create a map describing what their lives can be like if they remain sober.

DIRECTIONS: ▶

Give group members large sheets of newsprint and a variety of colored markers. Starting with the present, ask group members to draw a time line describing their future living a sober life. Encourage them to dream, to envision how they want their lives to be, what they want to be doing, how they want to be feeling about themselves, what kind of people they want to be connected with. There are no limits here. When they have drawn this line as far into the future as they wish, ask them to draw another time line. This new time line foretells what their future would be like if they were to begin using chemicals again. Starting also at the present, they should draw this line in black and consider all the possible negative consequences of relapse, such as getting kicked out of school or out of the house, no money, jail, back to treatment, suicide (see following page for a sample time line).

When everyone has finished their time lines, use the remainder of the session to discuss their drawings. If there isn't enough time to do this, you may wish to use another session for the second half of this activity.

MATERIALS: ▶

Newsprint and markers.

MY SOBER FUTURE Drawing Example

CLEAN AND SOBER

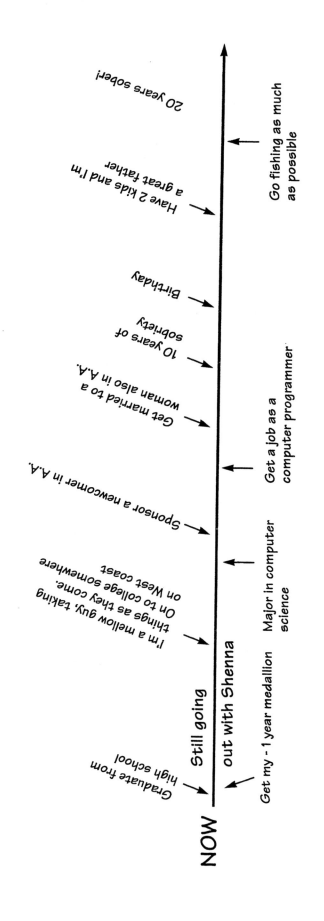

NOW

Graduate from high school

Still going out with Shenna

Get my - 1 year medallion

I'm a mellow guy, taking things as they come. On to college somewhere on West coast

Major in computer science

Sponsor a newcomer in A.A.

Get married to a woman also in A.A.

Get a job as a computer programmer

10 years of sobriety

Birthday

Have 2 kids and I'm a great father!

Go fishing as much as possible

20 years sober!

USING CHEMICALS

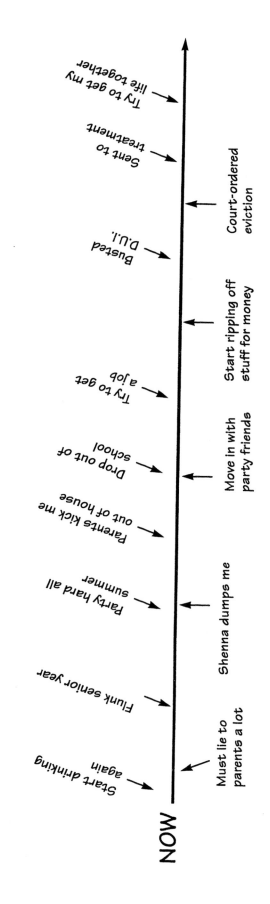

NOW

Start drinking again

Must lie to parents a lot

Flunk senior year

Shenna dumps me

Party hard all summer

Parents kick me out of house

Drop out of school

Move in with party friends

Try to get a job

Start ripping off stuff for money

Busted D.U.I.

Court-ordered eviction

Sent to treatment

Try to get my life together

29
Ten Different Feelings

GOALS: ▶
- ■ Identify personal defenses
- ■ Encourage discussion of secret feelings

DESCRIPTION: ▶ Group members use a worksheet to categorize feelings that are easy to share with others and feelings that are difficult to share with others.

DIRECTIONS: ▶ Ask group members to list some feelings that are easy to talk about; then ask them to list feelings that are really hard to talk about. Once familiar with this distinction, pass out the **Ten Different Feelings** worksheet (see following page). After they've had time to complete the worksheet, go around the circle and ask group members to share what they've written. Time permitting, ask them to relate an instance when they used a defense to cover up a feeling listed on their worksheet.

MATERIALS: ▶ **Ten Different Feelings** worksheet.

Ten Different Feelings

In the blanks provided, write in ten different feelings.

Then next to each feeling word you wrote, tell why the feeling is easy or difficult to talk about with other people.

■ Five feelings easy for me to talk about with others are:

1: _____

2: _____

3: _____

4: _____

5: _____

■ Five feelings difficult for me to talk about with others are:

1: _____

2: _____

3: _____

4: _____

5: _____

30
Feelings Card Game

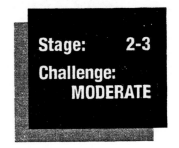

GOALS: ▶
- ■ Increase awareness of feelings
- ■ Develop communication skills

DESCRIPTION: ▶ Students select feelings cards representing their personality.

DIRECTIONS: ▶ This game uses the cards that come in the **Stamp Game** kit (see Resources section). Lay out the feelings cards in stacks in the center of the group circle. Call on group members to explain each of the eight feelings listed on the cards. Now ask students to take any number of cards from the piles to demonstrate the feelings they have inside. For example, a student might have a large pile of angry cards, a few guilt cards and one fear card. After group members have had time to build their stack of cards, ask them to discuss their stack of cards with the group by explaining why, for example, they have so many angry cards and what the fear cards are for. Additional game variations are provided in the **Stamp Game** kit.

NOTES: ▶ It is also possible to make your own set of feelings cards by cutting out cards from various colors of stiff paper and writing feelings words on them. You may wish to make this a group project.

MATERIALS: ▶ **Stamp Game** kit (see Resources section).

31
Five Familiar Feelings

Stage: 2-3
Challenge: MODERATE

GOALS:

- Identify connection between feelings and behaviors
- Pinpoint troublesome feelings

DESCRIPTION:

Group members describe specific situations that produce certain feelings and what they do with those feelings.

DIRECTIONS:

Begin a discussion focusing on feelings by asking everyone in the group to name a particular feeling that he or she has a difficult time handling. Point out to them that this is natural. Everyone handles some feelings better than others. Some people can't deal with loneliness well; others get all bent out of shape when they are feeling angry.

Pass out the **Five Familiar Feelings** worksheet (see following page) for group members to complete. When they are finished, spend the remaining time discussing their answers. Be sure to ask for specific examples. Jeanette might have written that when she's feeling lonely she doesn't know what to do with herself. By your insisting that she identify specific examples, she will begin to realize that it's when she's lonely that she ends up drunk and perhaps being sexual with some guy she barely knows. It is the specific, not the general, that will begin to make inroads into the confusion group members often feel.

MATERIALS:

Five Familiar Feelings worksheet.

Five Familiar Feelings

For each of the five feelings below, first describe a typical situation which would lead to that feeling. Then give a helpful and a harmful example of what you might do when you are feeling that way.

I feel happy when _____

When I'm feeling happy I . . .

Helpful: _____

Harmful: _____

I feel sad when _____

When I'm feeling sad I . . .

Helpful: _____

Harmful: _____

I feel angry when _____

When I'm feeling angry I . . .

Helpful: _____

Harmful: _____

I feel bored when _____

When I'm feeling bored I . . .

Helpful: _____

Harmful: _____

I feel lonely when _____

When I'm feeling lonely I . . .

Helpful: _____

Harmful: _____

32
What Should I Do with My Feelings?

GOALS:
- Explore different ways to cope with feelings
- Increase awareness of the variety of feelings

DESCRIPTION:
Group members identify feelings that they struggle with. The group then discusses different strategies to manage these feelings.

DIRECTIONS:
Ask each group member to think of a particular feeling that he or she finds difficult to handle. Ask them to write this feeling on a slip of paper, along with a personal example. Collect these papers, mix them up, draw a slip from the pile and read it out loud. Ask everyone in turn to explain how they deal with this particular feeling, giving examples from their personal lives. After all have shared, read the next slip of paper and continue the activity in likewise fashion.

NOTES:
Don't be afraid to point out additional methods for dealing with feelings if the group fails to mention strategies you think are important.

MATERIALS:
Slips of paper.

33
Head Games

GOALS: ▶

- Help students identify negative thinking patterns
- Teach students how to give themselves positive messages

DESCRIPTION: ▶

Students discuss common examples of negative thoughts and turn them around into positive messages.

DIRECTIONS: ▶

Give each group member several 3 x 5 inch index cards and ask them to write a negative thought that they sometimes tell themselves, such as, "I'll never get it right," "What's the use," "I'm so ugly," "Everyone else has lots of friends, except for me." Mix these cards up and put them in a pile facedown in the center of the group circle. Ask someone to draw the top card and read it out loud. Going around the circle, ask members to describe a time when they have told themselves a similar message. When everyone has done this, ask the group to replace this negative self-talk with a different, positive message. For example, if the negative self-talk is "I'm stupid," the positive message could be "It's okay to not know how to do everything—besides, I'm good at lots of other things." Ask members of the group for other positive examples before moving on to the next card in the pile.

MATERIALS: ▶

Index cards.

34
The Grieving Process

GOALS:

- Teach the stages of grieving
- Prepare students for possible grief reactions connected to when they quit using chemicals

DESCRIPTION: ▶

Students learn about the stages of the grieving process and discuss their grief reactions due to abstaining from mind-altering chemicals.

DIRECTIONS: ▶

Begin this session by making a presentation conveying the five stages of the grieving process (see following page for more information). Make certain they all understand this process by asking the group to describe possible grief reactions for a hypothetical loss that the group invents, such as a family member dying.

When this concept and its stages are well understood by the group, ask them to consider their own grief reactions to letting go of chemicals. For most group members, their relationship with alcohol and other drugs was extremely important, often described as a love affair with drugs. For example, Ken is angry (anger stage) that he can't use any longer, especially when he sees his friends going off to a party. Nancy sometimes wrestles with whether she even needs to quit, wondering if maybe she could just drink beer instead of smoking pot (bargaining stage).

Once you have given them a few minutes to contemplate this, use the remaining time to share these grief reactions.

MATERIALS:

None required.

For Your Information . . .

Grief is a reaction to heartfelt losses. Probably the first example that comes to mind is the death of a loved one, but there are many other examples, such as moving away, leaving adolescence, ending a relationship.

Young people who abuse alcohol and other drugs do so for myriad reasons, but it's safe to say that the mind-altering chemicals do something for them, be it making them feel popular, attractive, happy. And because alcohol and other drugs do this, chemically dependent people develop a love affair—a love affair with alcohol and other drugs. When they end this relationship, they will grieve the loss of identity, a group of friends, rituals, excitement, pleasure. Of course, they don't really lose these things—it just feels like it. Just as someone grieving over a divorce often feels there will never be anyone else in his life. It's important for young people struggling to quit using alcohol and other drugs to understand that it's normal for them to grieve the loss of this drug-centered life-style.

Grieving has stages first identified by Elizabeth Kübler-Ross in her work with dying patients. Listed below are these five stages and the thoughts typical of someone who has been diagnosed terminally ill with cancer:

Denial "No, it can't be true. I've just got the flu."
Anger "These quack doctors don't know anything."
Bargaining "I'll take my pills, but I'm never going to go through chemotherapy."
Depression "What's the use in trying."
Acceptance "I've got cancer but I'm going to enjoy every day I've got left."

A teenager who's just quit using chemicals might have this to say:

Denial "I don't have a problem."
Anger "It's not fair that I can't use any more!"
Bargaining "Well, I'll stay sober, but I'm not going to any of those A.A. meetings."
Depression "My life is so boring without parties."
Acceptance "As long as I stay clean and sober, I'm going to graduate from high school!"

These stages are experienced in sequence, and it's common to return to a stage previously experienced. A young person might vacillate between denial, anger, and bargaining for a long time before moving into the bottom two stages. She might even jump back up into the top three briefly again. Grieving students will work through these stages differently and at their own pace.

35
Assessment of Losses

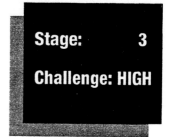

Stage: 3

Challenge: HIGH

GOALS:

- Encourage self-assessment of personal affects of chemical use
- Help students connect their behavior with consequences

DESCRIPTION: ▶

Students list the various losses they have experienced in their personal lives due to their prior chemical use.

DIRECTIONS: ▶

Begin this session by asking group members to give examples of famous people—actors, sports heroes, politicians—who have experienced tragedy due to their alcohol or other drug use. Usually most every group member can cite an example of a football star who was cut from the team because of drugs, or some other famous person who died in an alcohol-related car crash.

Point out to them that although these are rather infamous examples, all of the group, too, has experienced losses, such as the loss of a friend, a boyfriend, self-esteem, or trust from parents. Hand out the **My Own Losses** worksheet on the following page and, after giving them enough time to finish, spend the rest of the session discussing their answers.

MATERIALS:

My Own Losses worksheet.

My Own Losses

Many people experience losses due directly to their own chemical use. Some of these are tragically obvious—car crashes, dumped by a girlfriend or boyfriend, being fired—but other losses are not so clear. Consider each question listed below carefully before answering. Explain your answers instead of simply answering "yes" or "no."

1. Have you ever lost a job because of your chemical use?

2. Have you ever lost a boyfriend or girlfriend because of your chemical use?

3. Have you ever been physically or sexually abused while using chemicals?

4. Have you ever lost a friend because of your chemical use?

5. How has your chemical use affected your . . .

   ■ self-esteem

   ■ happiness

   ■ family relations

6. List three activities you no longer do because of your chemical use.

   1)

   2)

   3)

36
Signs and Symptoms of Chemical Dependence

GOALS:

- Increase understanding of the various signs and symptoms of chemical dependence
- Encourage students to look for these signs and symptoms in their past chemical use

DESCRIPTION: ▶

Group members choose specific signs and symptoms of chemical dependence from a list and discuss their relevance to their own lives.

DIRECTIONS: ▶

Point out to the group that, just as the common cold has a specific set of symptoms that tell us we've got one, so does chemical dependence have symptoms. Ask group members for a few examples of some of the more common symptoms of chemical dependence, such as getting drunk regularly, dropping out of school, entering a treatment program.

Hand out copies of the list of signs and symptoms (see following page). Pick a student to begin and ask her to choose a symptom from the list, read it out loud, and then choose another group member to respond to the question of whether or not he has experienced this particular symptom, as well as offering a personal example. Once he has answered the question, the rest of the group, proceeding in turn around the circle, should also answer this question. The person who first answered the question should continue the discussion by picking another symptom from the list and someone else to begin the discussion. Continue in this fashion for the entire group session.

Have enough copies of the signs and symptoms list so that everybody will have a copy to read. When a single list is passed around the circle, time is lost while group members choose from the list.

MATERIALS: ▶

Signs and Symptoms of Chemical Dependence List.

Signs and Symptoms of Chemical Dependence List

1. Increase in the amount of alcohol or other drugs used.
2. Arrested for MIP (Minor in Possession) offense.
3. Dramatic change in mood when drinking or using.
4. Denial of any problem.
5. Dishonesty with peers about drinking or using.
6. Failed attempts to quit or cut down on chemical use.
7. Association with known heavy users.
8. Frequent excuses for chemical use.
9. Protecting supply of chemicals.
10. Low self-image.
11. Hangovers or bad trips.
12. School suspension because of chemical use.
13. Frequent mood changes.
14. Deterioration of school grades.
15. Stealing money for chemicals.
16. Using chemicals while alone.
17. Loss of control while using or drinking.
18. Health problems.
19. Suicidal thoughts or behaviors.
20. Dropped by girlfriend or boyfriend because of chemical use.
21. Violent behavior when high or drunk.
22. Preoccupation with chemicals.
23. Increase in frequency of chemical use.
24. Increase in tolerance.
25. Memory loss.
26. Using chemicals in the morning.
27. Loss of friends.
28. Frequent broken promises.
29. Defensive when confronted.
30. Fired from jobs.
31. Going in for a chemical dependence evaluation.
32. Entering a chemical dependence treatment program.

37
Consequences of Chemical Use

GOALS:

- Remind students about the negative aspects of their previous chemical use
- Encourage honest self-examination

DESCRIPTION:

Students compile a list of typical consequences for chemical abuse and then identify which consequences they have experienced.

DIRECTIONS: ►

Using the blackboard, ask students to list consequences of chemical abuse. This list should be both comprehensive and specific, including examples such as getting kicked off the team for drinking, grounded at home because of going to a beer party, losing a girlfriend or boyfriend because of crazy behavior while drunk.

When there is a comprehensive list, ask students in turn to share with the rest of the group the consequences that they've experienced. It's important they also explain the chemical-related behavior that precipitated the consequence—in other words, not just the fact that they got arrested, but what they were doing that caused them to get arrested.

If a student is hesitant to openly share her personal consequences, you might ask the rest of the group to list, in a good-natured manner, several consequences they know this person has experienced.

MATERIALS: ►

None required.

38
What's Different Now?

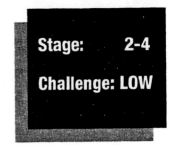

GOALS: ▶
- Clarify importance of sobriety
- Help students recognize what is different now that they don't use chemicals

DESCRIPTION: ▶
Students compare and contrast the differences in their lives before and after they quit using alcohol and other drugs.

DIRECTIONS: ▶
Ask the group to close their eyes and think back to when they were in trouble because of their chemical use. Prompt them to remember the feelings and consequences they experienced. After a few minutes of reflecting, bring them back to the present by asking them to think about how things are going now. Spend the remainder of the session discussing these differences.

QUESTIONS: ▶
- Has your life improved since you quit using alcohol and other drugs?
- What's different now?
- Do other people, such as family and friends, notice these differences?
- What hasn't changed since you've quit using alcohol and other drugs?
- Would you like these things to change or remain the same?

MATERIALS: ▶
None required.

39
School and Sobriety

GOALS:
- Discuss problems concerning abstinence and school attendance
- Discuss constructive alternatives

DESCRIPTION: ▶

Students discuss the difficulties of staying sober while attending school and consider possible solutions.

DIRECTIONS: ▶

Ask the group to make a list on the blackboard of all the problems they've experienced staying sober while attending school, such as hassles with former friends who still get high, teachers who don't understand their need for an ongoing support group, or not being able to get rid of their former reputation as a "burnout." Encourage them to vent their frustrations.

When the list is finished, ask them to think of solutions for each item on the list. For example, instead of being tempted by former friends to get high during lunch break, group members could eat lunch together. If there is a problem with teachers not understanding the importance of the support group, group members could make a brief presentation about what it's like coming back to school after being in a treatment center to the staff during their staff meeting.

When each item on the blackboard has been addressed, finish up this session by pointing out to the group that there are some positive aspects to attending school, such as their support group, recreational activities, and contact with friends who are also staying clean and sober. Ask them to think of and discuss other benefits that their school has to offer.

MATERIALS:

None required.

40
Romance and Relationships

Stage: 2-3
Challenge: MODERATE

GOALS:

- Help students work towards healthy relationships
- Focus on importance of placing sobriety before romantic relationships

DESCRIPTION: ▶

Students make a list of warning signs in regard to unhealthy relationships and then apply this list to their own relationships.

DIRECTIONS: ▶

Begin this session by asking the group to describe examples of how a romantic relationship can jeopardize their sobriety, such as skipping twelve-step meetings to be with a girlfriend or going out driving around with a boyfriend who's drinking some beers.

Once it's clearly established that romantic encounters can sometimes jeopardize their sobriety, ask group members how they would know if they were in this kind of relationship. As they begin to voice some ideas, ask the group to put together a list of warning signs by appointing a group member to record everyone's ideas. Typical examples can include missing meetings to be with this person, spending less time working a personal recovery program, defending your girlfriend's right to drink even though you're concerned she might have a problem with chemicals, not telling your boyfriend that you're recovering from chemical dependence.

Once this warning signs list is finished, give everyone a sheet of paper to record their answers to the warning list the group has constructed. You may wish to read the warning list aloud to the group, asking them to write a yes or a no for each item. Afterwords, ask group members to add up their yes answers and use the remaining time to discuss their scores and the implications.

QUESTIONS:

- What was your score?
- What does this score tell you?
- Do you think that your romantic relationships jeopardize your sobriety? Why or why not?
- What could you change to make your relationship more supportive of your sobriety?

NOTES:

Most likely, there'll be members of the group who aren't currently involved in a romantic relationship. In this case ask them to use a past relationship when answering questions on the test.

MATERIALS:

Paper.

41
Body Language

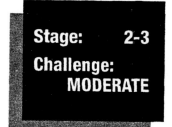

GOALS: ▶
- Create awareness of body language
- Encourage students to examine their own body language

DESCRIPTION: ▶

Students act out common feelings using body language while the rest of the group attempts to identify the feeling.

DIRECTIONS: ▶

Make a set of feelings cards on 3 x 5 inch index cards or construction paper (see following page for a list of feelings). Before beginning the game, ask the group for examples of how we communicate feelings without using the spoken language, such as gestures, body position, amount of eye contact.

Play this game by asking a student to select a card from the facedown pile of feelings cards and to act out the feeling for the rest of the group. As in the game of charades, this student shouldn't use any words. First he should rely solely on body language as he acts out the feeling for the rest of the group. If they can't identify the feeling, then he could also add sounds, such as a sigh, grunt, or whistle. When the group guesses the feeling correctly, stop the game briefly and ask everyone to tell the rest of the group how the group would know when he or she is feeling that particular feeling. For example, John might get very quiet and noncommunicative when he's angry; Sarah might become agitated and aggressive when she's angry. Once everyone has shared how they respond to the named feeling, continue the game with a new card and actor.

MATERIALS: ▶

Feelings cards.

Feelings List

afraid	eager	joyful	scared
aggressive	enraged	lonely	secure
alarmed	enthusiastic	loved	shocked
amused	envious	mad	surprised
angry	exasperated	miserable	tense
annoyed	excited	needed	terrified
anxious	frightened	nervous	threatened
appreciated	frustrated	paranoid	thrilled
bitter	furious	perplexed	troubled
bored	glad	powerful	uneasy
calm	guilty	powerless	unimportant
cautious	happy	puzzled	unloved
comfortable	helpless	regretful	unneeded
concerned	horrified	rejected	unsure
confident	hostile	relieved	wanted
confused	hurt	resentful	worried
contented	inadequate	respected	worthless
crushed	insecure	sad	worthwhile
disappointed	irritated	safe	
discouraged	jealous	satisfied	

42
Junk Food Junkies

Stage: 2-3

Challenge: LOW

GOALS: ▶
- Establish a connection between diet and emotional health
- Encourage students to analyze their own eating habits

DESCRIPTION: ▶

Students discuss their eating habits and how this affects their emotional and physical health.

DIRECTIONS: ▶

Place a collection of empty junk-food containers in the center of the group circle, such as pop cans, candy wrappers, and potato chip bags. Ask a group member to begin the activity by taking items from the center that are reflective of his diet and placing them in front of him. Then ask him to describe what he eats during a typical day. After he's finished, ask the rest of the group what it thinks about his diet—"Hey, you eat way too much sugar!" or "That's great that you eat breakfast everyday; I never do," for example. After he's finished, ask him to pick another group member to go next.

QUESTIONS: ▶
- What's healthy about your diet? What's not so healthy?
- How long have you been eating this way?
- What should you change about your diet?
- What are you willing to change about your diet?
- Will this change be hard to make?
- What are the benefits of this change?

MATERIALS: ▶

Collection of empty junk-food containers.

43
Messages About Chemical Use

GOALS: ▶
- Increase awareness of manipulation by media
- Identify societal messages concerning chemical use

DESCRIPTION: ▶ Students make collages of ads that influence their attitudes about using chemicals.

DIRECTIONS: ▶ Place a large pile of general-interest magazines in the center of the group circle along with enough scissors and bottles of glue for everyone. Give everyone a sheet of newsprint and ask them to page through the magazines, cutting out advertisements and other messages that address chemical use. These messages may be either positive or negative. They should use these cutouts to make a collage that reflects their impressions of societal messages about chemical use. Save some time at the end of the session to discuss the collages, asking students to explain their collages to the rest of the group.

QUESTIONS: ▶
- What messages are we given about chemical use?
- Do the messages differ according to the chemical?
- Which of these messages are true? Which are false?
- Do these messages affect your attitudes or behaviors?
- How do these messages affect your ability to stay clean and sober?

NOTES: ▶ Talking about these collages is the important part of this activity. It's common for students to want to work on their collages right up to the end of the session, but you must save some time for discussion—even if they haven't finished yet. It's a good idea to sound a ten- and five-minute warning as they approach the end of the time available for working on the collages.

MATERIALS: ▶ Magazines, scissors, glue.

44
My Day by the Slice

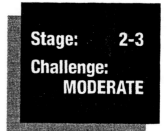

GOALS: ▶
- Assess amount of time devoted to working a recovery program
- Encourage students to review how they use their time.

DESCRIPTION: ▶
Students complete a worksheet that details how they spend their time.

DIRECTIONS: ▶
Begin this session by asking group members for examples of activities they usually do during the day. Encourage them to list as many as they can think of, everything from sleeping to watching TV, from eating to driving around, from going to twelve-step meetings to seeing a counselor. You may wish to ask them to make a list of these activities on the blackboard to refer to during the second part of this activity.

Pass out the **Time Wheel** worksheet (see following page) and crayons or colored pencils. When everyone has finished, ask everyone to give their worksheet to the person on their right. When everyone has a different group member's worksheet, ask group members to describe their neighbor's time wheel to the group.

QUESTIONS: ▶
- What conclusions can you draw after looking at your neighbor's Time Wheel? What does she spend the most time doing? The least?
- What percentage of the **Time Wheel** do twelve-step groups and other recovery-related activities occupy?
- Should she make any changes in her personal schedule?

MATERIALS: ▶
Time Wheel worksheet, crayons or colored pencils.

Time Wheel

Write activities typical of a day in your life in separate areas of the wheel. Make the size of the sections represent how much time is spent for each particular activity. Fill each area in with a different color. For example, if you generally sleep eight hours, then color eight sections of the circle blue and label it "sleeping."

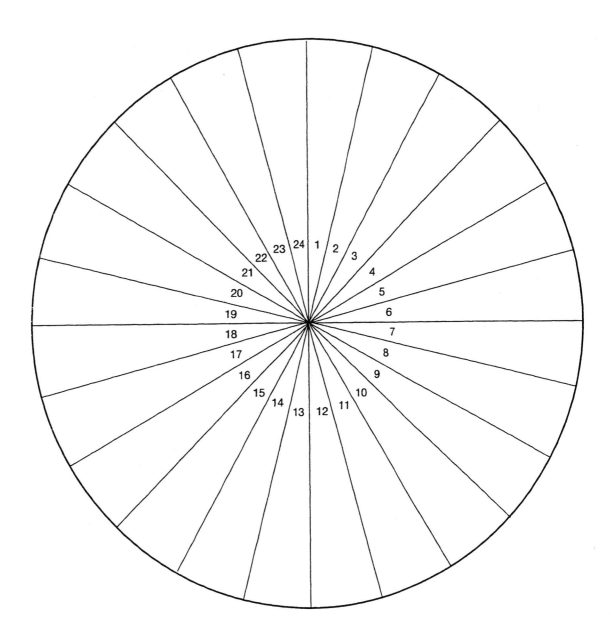

45
Personality Profile

GOALS: ▶
- Identify personality traits
- Help students understand their personality

DESCRIPTION: ▶ Students complete a worksheet that helps them understand the strengths and weaknesses of their personalities.

DIRECTIONS: ▶ Begin this session by challenging group members to describe their personalities. Most likely they will struggle with this, as it's a difficult task for all of us.

Explain to the group that despite the difficulty of describing our personalities, this is an important issue to deal with. We all need to know about ourselves. Are we outgoing or reserved, happy or sad, lonely or the life of the party, quick to anger or easygoing?

Give everyone a copy of the **Personality Profile** worksheet (see following page) to complete. Once they have finished, spend the remaining time discussing their answers.

QUESTIONS: ▶
- Has your personality always been like it is now?
- If it has changed, when and why?
- Are you happy with your personality now?
- What would you change?
- How could you go about changing your personality?

MATERIALS: ▶ **Personality Profile** worksheet.

Personality Profile

Consider each set of opposite traits below and circle the number that best describes you. Once you have scored the fifteen traits, connect your circles with a line from top to bottom.

calm	1	2	3	4	5	6	nervous
popular	1	2	3	4	5	6	loner
expressive	1	2	3	4	5	6	inhibited
caring	1	2	3	4	5	6	indifferent
aggressive	1	2	3	4	5	6	compliant
patient	1	2	3	4	5	6	impatient
self-disciplined	1	2	3	4	5	6	impulsive
trustworthy	1	2	3	4	5	6	untrustworthy
happy	1	2	3	4	5	6	sad
honest	1	2	3	4	5	6	dishonest
confident	1	2	3	4	5	6	insecure
mellow	1	2	3	4	5	6	angry
abstinent	1	2	3	4	5	6	heavy user
self-aware	1	2	3	4	5	6	unaware
motivated	1	2	3	4	5	6	procrastinator

46
Tombstone Talk

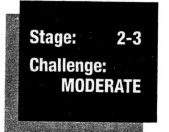

Stage: 2-3
Challenge: MODERATE

GOALS: ▶
- Help students clarify their personal values
- Identify which personal qualities they value most

DESCRIPTION: ▶
Students discuss how they would like to be remembered after they die.

DIRECTIONS: ▶
Pass out sheets of newsprint and markers and ask group members to draw a large outline of a gravestone, such as a rectangle or an upside-down "U." In the top of this marker, they should write something like "Here lies" and their name. Before they fill in the rest of the stone, ask them to stop for a minute and think about how they would like to be remembered when they are dead. Would they want people to say, "Oh, that Jim was such a joketeller," or "Lenore always was helpful to those around her"?

Once they have an idea of how they would want people to remember them, they should write these quotations and descriptions on their tombstones. When everyone is finished, ask them to explain their tombstones to the rest of the group.

QUESTIONS: ▶
- What would you want people to say about you after you're dead?
- How would you want to be remembered after you're dead?
- If you were to die today, is this how they would remember you?
- If not, what do you need to change or work on?

MATERIALS: ▶
Newsprint and markers.

47
My Story

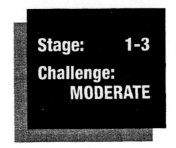

GOALS: ▶
- Share personal history with the group
- Encourage intimacy within the group

DESCRIPTION: ▶
Students explain their past struggles with chemical dependence to the rest of the group and what events led them to this support group.

DIRECTIONS: ▶
An excellent method for encouraging connections between group members and for the group to experience a common bond is to ask everyone to share their personal story, or what has lead them to this support group. Some group members might already be familiar with the format of this activity because it's similar to a common topic in twelve-step meetings: "What it was like, what happened, and what it's like now."

As this can be a rather drawn-out affair, you may wish to do this activity over a course of weeks, one group member taking a turn every week at the beginning of each session to share her story.

QUESTIONS: ▶
- What was it like for you when you were using chemicals?
- How was your emotional and family life then?
- Was there some sort of crisis that helped you quit? What was it?
- What is your life like now?

NOTES: ▶
Whenever a new student begins the support group, it's a good idea to ask him to share his story with the rest of the group. This will help the group feel more comfortable and accepting of the new member, as well as help the new member feel included.

MATERIALS: ▶
None required.

48
"I Am" Creed

GOALS: ▶
- Encourage students to value themselves
- Instill a habit of reflecting on personal worth

DESCRIPTION: ▶ Students read the **"I Am" Creed** out loud at the beginning of a group session.

DIRECTIONS: ▶ Ask a group member to read the **"I Am" Creed** out loud (see following page). When she's finished, ask group members to discuss their reactions to this creed. Some may think it's stupid to talk to yourself in this manner; other group members may have a hard time believing these things about themselves. Point out to the group that it's important they treat themselves with dignity and respect. After all, they're important just for who they are, regardless of what they do or accomplish. Ask the group, "If you won't stand by yourself, then who will?"

NOTES: ▶ You may find it helpful to read this creed at the beginning of every group session. Though it may seem awkward at first, repeating the creed over and over again will help group members begin to believe its message.

MATERIALS: ▶ **"I Am" Creed.**

"I Am" Creed

I am because I am alive.

I am because there's no one around just like me.

I have great qualities and some not-so-great qualities.

I laugh, I understand, I hurt, I play, I get angry, I have special talents, I can make things, do things.

I am a special, unique collection of all that's life.

I am a recipe that will never be repeated.

I am not you nor anyone else.

I am me.

Section C:
Family Relations Activities

Even though teenagers are quick to point out they aren't a child any longer, group members' families continue to have much impact on their attitudes, feelings, and behaviors. And the reality is, even though group members are now recovering, their families might not be. Perhaps they are still reeling from the devastating affects of their son or daughter's active chemical dependence, such as the endless lies, verbal abuse when their teenage son came home drunk, or calls from the police and school. After all, just because their son or daughter went through treatment and hasn't used any chemicals for a month or two doesn't erase five years of crazy, painful behavior and family discord.

Maybe one of the parents is still actively chemically dependent. This common situation makes it especially tough for a teenager struggling with her own chemical dependence to stay abstinent because of the lack of support or even outright sabotage by the rest of the family still caught up in the family dysfunction.

Regardless of familial background, group members will quickly discover their family relationships will be the last area in their lives to improve. During group they will complain about the lack of trust, overprotectiveness, poor communication, and tension they are still experiencing at home. The activities in this section will help them to better understand these family dynamics and provide them with the tools they need to do their part in repairing the damage that they've helped create.

49
Family Collage

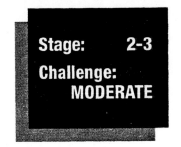
GOALS: ▶
- Describe students' families
- Explore feelings related to family issues

DESCRIPTION: ▶
Students make a collage depicting their families and family issues using pictures cut from magazines.

DIRECTIONS: ▶
Place a large stack of diverse magazines in the center of the group circle. After giving everyone scissors, glue, and a sheet of construction paper, ask group members to page through the magazines and cut out pictures or words that describe their families, the problems their families experience, and the students' reaction to their families. They can either paste on pictures and words as they find them, or first cut out all of the pictures they will use and then begin to assemble the collage. Once the collages are finished, the remaining time can be spent discussing them.

QUESTIONS: ▶
- What kind of feelings are represented in your collage?
- What are the problems in your family?
- What would you change in your family?
- Where are you in your collage?

NOTES: ▶
You may wish to make this activity span two sessions—the first for making the collage and the second for group discussion.

MATERIALS: ▶
Wide variety of magazines representing cultural diversity, sheets of construction paper, scissors, and bottles of white glue.

50
Family Faces

GOALS: ▶
- Increase awareness of family dynamics
- Assess specific relationships within students' families

DESCRIPTION: ▶
Students complete a worksheet by drawing expressive faces for, and describing the relationship with, each member of their families.

DIRECTIONS: ▶
Hand out the **Family Faces** worksheet (see following page) and ask them to draw expressive features for each blank face. When they are finished with the faces, they should follow the instructions for the blank lines next to each face. When everyone has finished the worksheet, ask them to share their answers with the rest of the group.

QUESTIONS: ▶
- Do the moods of your family members change often? Why is this?
- Can you read the differing moods of your family?
- Which family members do you feel close to? Which ones are difficult for you to spend time with?

NOTES: ▶
When students are living with a stepparent, they might ask, for example, if they should designate their biological father or their stepfather (or Mom's live-in boyfriend) as "Dad." Instruct them to make their own choices, but to place the person they didn't select as "Dad" in the "other family" section of the worksheet.

MATERIALS: ▶
Family Faces worksheet.

Family Faces

FAMILY FACES

	words that describe this person	words that describe your feelings about this person

MOM

( )
_____
_____
_____

DAD

( )
_____
_____
_____

BROTHERS & SISTERS

( )
_____
_____
_____

( )
_____
_____
_____

( )
_____
_____
_____

OTHER FAMILY

( )
_____
_____
_____

( )
_____
_____
_____

51
Family Trees

GOALS: ▶
- Create understanding of generational legacy of chemical dependence
- Increase understanding of dysfunctional family dynamics

DESCRIPTION: ▶

Students draw a Family Tree depicting past generations and relatives who had drinking or other drug problems.

DIRECTIONS: ▶

Begin this session by asking group members to raise a hand if they have a relative with a drinking or other drug problem. Probably most will raise a hand.

Hand out sheets of newsprint and tell the group that you would like them to map out the effects of chemical dependence on their extended families by drawing a Family Tree. Starting with both sets of grandparents, ask group members to use lines to connect parents and children through the generations until they reach the present.

Once this outline is complete, ask them to identify any relatives and immediate family members who've had a problem with alcohol or other drugs by drawing a heavy line around the person's name and writing a few words to describe the problem, such as alcoholic, smokes pot, or takes sleeping pills. Once this is done, finish the family tree by drawing a heavy line that connects all of these people who have had a problem with chemicals.

The rest of the session should be used to discuss the family trees. Point out to group members that their sobriety marks an important change in their families—they are putting a stop to the disease of chemical dependence being passed on through each successive generation.

QUESTIONS: ▶
- Does your family discuss other relatives' drinking problems?
- Is anyone else in your family recovering?
- How does it feel to be the first family member to do something about this problem?
- Does your extended family support your sobriety? What do they tell you?

NOTES: ▶

Occasionally you'll have a group member who doesn't have any family members who have had a problem with chemicals. In this case, encourage them to draw a Family Tree and describe some of the personality traits of family members, or some of the unhealthy rules that are passed down through the generations, such as not talking about feelings or expressing anger physically. Also remind group members that sometimes chemical dependence skips a generation, so it isn't uncommon for a grandparent to be chemically dependent but not the student's parents.

MATERIALS: ▶

Newsprint and markers.

52
Does the Problem Affect Me?

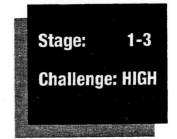

GOALS: ▶
- Help students understand family dysfunction
- Encourage honest appraisal of a chemical dependence problem
- Increase group unity

DESCRIPTION: ▶

Group members complete a short questionnaire that focuses on how children are affected by a parent's chemical dependence. The remainder of the session is spent discussing the group members' answers.

DIRECTIONS: ▶

Pass out the questionnaires (see following page) and ask students to answer each question honestly. Remind them that since chemical dependence tends to run in families, it wouldn't be very surprising if there is someone else in their family who is also chemically dependent. After everyone has finished, ask students to share their answers with the rest of the group.

NOTES: ▶

Being mindful of the time remaining, ask group members for examples rather than simply "yes" or "no" answers. For example, with question #1 you could ask, "Why are you concerned?" or "What bothers you about this person's drinking?"

This activity will be more successful if you call first on students who are already able to make an honest appraisal of the chemical dependence problem in their families. This will encourage other group members to share honestly.

MATERIALS: ▶

Questionnaire.

Questionnaire

PLEASE CHECK YES OR NO TO THE FOLLOWING QUESTIONS:

	YES	NO
1. Are you concerned about a parent's, relative's, or close friend's chemical use?	__	__
2. Do you spend a lot of time thinking about this person's chemical use?	__	__
3. Have you ever thought that this person has a problem with his or her chemical use?	__	__
4. Do you stay out of the house as much as possible because of this person's chemical use?	__	__
5. Are you afraid to upset this person because it may cause him or her to use more chemicals?	__	__
6. Do you feel that no one at home really loves you or cares what happens to you?	__	__
7. Are you afraid or embarrassed to bring your friends home because of a family member's chemical use?	__	__
8. Do you tell lies to cover up for this person's chemical use?	__	__
9. Have you ever wanted to talk to somebody about this person's chemical use?	__	__
10. Is your school work suffering because of this person's chemical use?	__	__

53
Parent Quiz

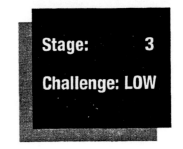

GOALS: ▶

- Increase students' understanding of their parents
- Encourage honest communication between students and their parents

DESCRIPTION: ▶

Students complete a quiz that indicates how well they know their parents.

DIRECTIONS: ▶

Ask the group how well they know their parents. Most likely they will say they know them all too well! Point out to them that we usually know our parents as parents, not as people with likes, dislikes, hurts, concerns, fears. Give group members a copy of the **Parent Quiz** (see following page). After they're finished, discuss the results by comparing scores as well as asking them once again, "How well do you know your parents?"

Ask group members to take their quizzes home and ask their parents these questions and discuss the answers. The following group session can be used to discuss what they learned from this experience.

QUESTIONS: ▶

- How well do you know your parents?
- How many questions on the quiz were you not able to answer?
- After talking with your parents, were some of your answers wrong? Which ones?
- Why don't you know your parents very well?
- How could you begin to get to know them better?

MATERIALS: ▶

Parent Quiz.

Parent Quiz

Complete this quiz based on what you know about your parents. If you don't know the answer to a question, leave it blank. **Don't guess**.

1. When are your parents' birthdays?
Mother _____
Father _____

2. Where were your parents born?
Mother _____
Father _____

3. What kind of students were your parents in high school?
Mother _____
Father _____

4. When your parents were your age, what did they argue about with their parents?
Mother _____
Father _____

5. Are your parents happy?
Mother _____
Father _____

6. Do your parents like what they do for a living?
Mother _____
Father _____

7. What's been the happiest moment in your parents' lives?
Mother _____
Father _____

8. What's been the saddest moment in your parents' lives?
Mother _____
Father _____

9. Do your parents ever cry?
Mother _____
Father _____

10. If your parents could change one thing about their lives, what would it be?
Mother _____
Father _____

54
Regaining Trust

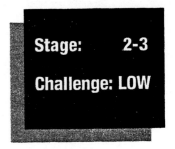
GOALS: ▶
- Help students connect past behavior with present consequences regarding lack of trust from parents
- Identify ways to regain this lost trust

DESCRIPTION: ▶

Students use a checklist to examine the level of trust between themselves and their parents and discuss ways to increase this trust level.

DIRECTIONS: ▶

Hand out copies of the **Trust Checklist** (see following page) to group members. Make sure they write additional examples of mistrust other than the examples on the checklist. When everyone has completed the top half of the checklist, discuss these examples. Most likely, many students will have similar answers. Now, for each example of mistrust, ask group members to explain why there is this mistrust. For example, a group member reports she can't stay home alone when her parents are gone for the weekend because she always had keg parties as soon as they left.

Once there's been a connection made between past behaviors involving chemical use and the current lack of trust, challenge the group to think of ways they could win back this trust. Typical examples will include staying sober, attending school regularly, being honest with their parents about what's going on in their lives, hanging around other recovering peers.

QUESTIONS: ▶
- What is the trust level between you and your parents?
- How did this trust level become so low?
- Would you like this trust level to increase?
- What can you do to help this process?

MATERIALS: ▶

Trust Checklist.

Trust Checklist

Signs of low trust levels: (check all that apply to you)

_____ Your parents must know where you are at all times.

_____ It's difficult or impossible to get the car.

_____ Your parents smell your breath for alcohol.

_____ Your parents won't leave you alone for the weekend.

_____ Your parents won't give you much money.

_____ Your parents double-check your stories.

_____ If something goes wrong, your parents assume the worst.

_____ Your parents keep you on a behavioral contract.

_____ Your parents often question you about your friends.

_____ Your parents have set an unreasonable curfew for you.

Write your own:

_____ _____

_____ _____

_____ _____

_____ _____

Here are some things I can do to begin winning back more trust:

_____

_____

_____

_____

_____

_____

_____

_____

55
A Letter to My Parent

GOALS: ▶
- Clarify problems and concerns students have concerning relationships with their parents
- Encourage expression of feelings

DESCRIPTION: ▶ Group members write a letter to their parents voicing their concerns and what they need. These letters aren't sent, but are destroyed in a ritualistic fashion.

DIRECTIONS: ▶ Ask group members to write a letter to either or both parents. After making sure they understand that these letters won't be sent to their parent, tell them to communicate all the things they would like to say but can't. This might include a group member telling her father how sorry she is for all the trouble she caused before she ended up in treatment, a group member telling his mother how worried he is about her drinking, or talking about how he wishes things could be at home. These letters will naturally be diverse and personal, but the key is for group members to express things they otherwise wouldn't be able to. When everyone is finished writing, ask students who are comfortable doing so to read their letters to the group.

There is a rather ceremonious and symbolic way to destroy these letters. After a student has read her letter—either out loud or to herself—ask her to fold the letter in half and rip it up. But for each rip of the folded letter, she should tell the group something she is doing or will start doing to take care of herself or correct the problem shared in the letter, such as talking about her feelings, avoiding arguing with her mother when her mother is drunk, or making sure she goes to her A.A. meeting regularly.

MATERIALS: ▶ Paper.

Section D:
Preventing Relapse Activities

Adolescents struggling to stay clean and sober need all the help we can provide. The tremendous peer pressure, impulsiveness, and vacillating emotions inherent to adolescence can topple the best of intentions to stay clean and sober, resulting in a slide back to the familiar, though destructive, coping behaviors of using mind-altering chemicals. This return to alcohol or other drugs is called a relapse.

Relapse is dangerous. A few people return to sobriety after a single episode of chemical use all the stronger in their decision to abstain. For most, though, a relapse is the start of an extended downward spiral, often requiring another intervention and treatment period. Some adolescents never get a second chance to recover. As Narcotics Anonymous points out: "Once is too many, and a thousand never enough."

Preventing a relapse *before* it occurs is the answer. And that's the focus of the activities in this section. Relapses don't "just happen." There are warning signs along the way. Likewise, there are things that can be done to help prevent a relapse from ever occurring. With the help of these activities, group members will begin to build a quality recovery program and be aware of their own danger areas. This will help prevent relapse as well as ensure a chemical-free life-style that's healthy and satisfying.

56
Sobriety Slogans

GOALS: ▶
- Reinforce important recovery concepts
- Provide tools students can use to stay sober

DESCRIPTION: ▶

Students list and discuss twelve-step program slogans that can help them make healthy choices and improve the quality of their sobriety.

DIRECTIONS: ▶

Since most of the members of the support group have attended twelve-step meetings before, many will have heard various slogans used during meetings. Ask the group to list the slogans they have previously heard. It will be helpful to write these slogans on the blackboard. Once the group has made a list, you can add to it using slogans from the following page.

Taking turns, ask group members to explain what the slogans mean so that all are familiar with these important concepts, reminders, and warnings. Use the remaining time in this session to ask group members to pick a slogan they particularly like, or one which they really need to practice in their lives. Ask them to explain why this slogan is meaningful to them.

MATERIALS: ▶

Sobriety Slogans List.

Sobriety Slogans List

■ **KISS (Keep it simple, stupid)**
If you're someone who is just beginning in recovery (and therefore "stupid") don't make matters complicated—just don't drink or get high, and go to lots of meetings.

■ **First things first**
Your sobriety must come first. Period. Without that, everything else will crumble.

■ **Easy does it**
Be gentle with yourself. Go slowly.

■ **Hugs, not drugs**
For many people with an alcohol or other drug problem, the drugs were a people substitute. Now it's time to get what you need from people: affection, attention, understanding, hugs.

■ **One day at a time**
Yesterday is gone, and tomorrow not yet here. Focus on taking care of things today and don't worry about tomorrow or kick yourself for mistakes made in the past.

■ **Let go and let God**
A reminder that we aren't in control of the big picture. Instead of trying to control other people and events, take care of yourself and let go of the rest.

■ **One is too many, and a thousand never enough**
One drink or joint is enough to set a chemically dependent person off on a binge of partying, yet all the drugs in the world won't really give him what he is looking for—happiness and peace of mind.

■ **Live and let live**
Concentrate on living your own life as best you can, and let other people take care of their lives. Mind your own business.

■ **HALT (Hungry, angry, lonely, or tired)**
If you're feeling hungry, angry, lonely, or tired, it's time to stop and take care of yourself before attempting anything that might be challenging.

■ **Each day a new beginning**
No matter how much you might have messed up yesterday, you can make a fresh start today.

■ **Expect a miracle**
Be optimistic about your life and what will come of it.

57
What's My Program?

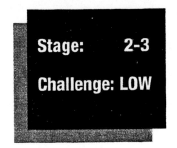

GOALS: ▶

- Clarify what students do to stay abstinent from alcohol and other drugs
- Pinpoint areas in students' recovery program that need improvement

DESCRIPTION: ▶

Students discuss the ingredients of a quality recovery program, and describe their own recovery programs.

DIRECTIONS: ▶

Using the blackboard, ask group members to list all the things someone newly clean and sober should be doing in order to make sure he or she doesn't drink or get high again. These activities, such as attending twelve-step meetings, working with a counselor, and going to aftercare, make up a person's recovery program.

Hand out copies of **My Recovery Program** worksheet (see following page). Once everyone has completed the worksheet, spend the remainder of the session discussing their answers.

QUESTIONS: ▶

- Are you satisfied with your recovery program?
- Does it help keep you clean and sober?
- Who made your recovery program—you, your parents, or your counselor?
- What would you like to change about your recovery program?

MATERIALS: ▶

My Recovery Program worksheet.

My Recovery Program

Your Recovery Program is all the things you do in order to stay clean and sober. How many of these are a part of your Recovery Program?

	Yes	No
■ Weekly A.A. or N.A. meetings	___	___
■ Daily meditation time	___	___
■ Working the twelve steps	___	___
■ Social contact with recovering peers	___	___
■ Regular time with sponsor	___	___
■ School support group	___	___
■ Aftercare group	___	___
■ Individual counseling or therapy	___	___

The ingredients of my Recovery Program:

1)

2)

3)

4)

5)

Two things I can do to make my Recovery Program better:

1)

2)

58
Seriously Sober, Conscientiously Clean

Stage: 3

Challenge: HIGH

GOALS: ▶
- Encourage students to examine their motivations for staying clean and sober
- Evaluate group members' sobriety

DESCRIPTION: ▶

Each student takes a turn being the center of attention while the rest of the group discusses how seriously he or she is about remaining sober and working a recovery program.

DIRECTIONS: ▶

Hand out sets of numbered cards to everyone in the group. The cards must be numbered from 1 to 10 and every student must have a complete set. You could make these cards with 3 x 5 inch index cards, or use several decks of playing cards, giving one suit, with the face cards removed, to each group member.

After someone has volunteered to begin this activity, ask the rest of the group to consider this person's sobriety and recovery program. Then everyone should choose a numbered card they think reflects this person's seriousness about staying clean and sober. A 1 means the student isn't serious at all about her sobriety; a 10 means she is working very hard at staying clean and sober. Once everyone has selected a card and placed it face down on his or her lap, ask group members, one at a time, to hold their cards up and explain why they chose that number. For example, Mario might have chosen a 4 because he thinks that Marianne is staying sober mostly because her boyfriend is, and that he doesn't ever see her going to meetings anymore. Beth might have chosen an 8 because she remembers how Marianne used to act and how much more mature and honest she is with her feelings now. Ask the group member who's being talked about to wait until all have shared their numbers and impressions before responding.

NOTES: ▶

This activity is geared towards examining group members' seriousness about staying clean and sober, not how likely they are to stay sober. While these two concepts might seem to be one and the same, they actually are not. One person might work very had at staying sober, but the odds are against him because of his family circumstances or pressures from his peer group. Another group member might adopt a lazy approach to recovery, yet have an easy time of sobriety because nobody in her family has a drinking problem and none of her friends drinks or gets high. We can't predict the future, but we can make observations concerning a group member's past and present behaviors and attitudes.

Also, you may wish to remove the 5s from the decks so that group members aren't allowed to "ride the fence" in their expressed opinions. Another rule you may wish to consider is to not allow group members to change cards once they've put a card face down. Sometimes, after seeing the number that other group members choose, group members who've not yet shared will change their card to be more in line with the rest of the group. Encourage them to be bold and stick by their impressions.

MATERIALS: ▶

Numbered cards.

59
Why I'm Staying Clean and Sober

GOALS:

■ Clarify personal reasons for remaining abstinent from alcohol and other drugs
■ Assert the positive value of sobriety

DESCRIPTION: ▶

Students discuss their individual reasons for staying clean and sober based on the worksheet they complete.

DIRECTIONS: ▶

Begin this session by pointing out to the group that, whether they realize it or not, they all have reasons for why they are staying clean and sober. Ask the group to make a list on the blackboard of all the reasons why someone would want to remain abstinent from alcohol and other drugs, such as it feels good, it's better for your body, gets your parents off your back, you can graduate from school, won't worry about getting busted.

After they've completed this list, hand out copies of the **Why I'm Staying Clean and Sober** worksheet (see following page). Once they've completed it, ask them to share their answers with the rest of the group. After someone has shared her list, ask the rest of the group for additional reasons why this group member should be staying clean and sober. For example, Sharon might list "Keep my parents off my case, get better grades, feel better about myself." Then the group reminds her that her boyfriend told her he wouldn't go out with her any longer if she started drinking again and that she would lose her job at the taco shop.

MATERIALS: ▶

Why I'm Staying Clean and Sober worksheet.

Why I'm Staying Clean and Sober

There are plenty of reasons for you to be staying abstinent from alcohol and other drugs. Which ones are important for you?

I'm staying clean and sober because:

1)

2)

3)

4)

5)

The rewards for me staying clean and sober are:

1)

2)

3)

4)

5)

60
Recovery
Recommendation

GOALS: ▶
- Clarify caregiver's recommendations
- Identify options for stable sobriety and personal growth

DESCRIPTION: ▶

Students discuss what has been recommended for them by their caregivers in order to ensure continuous sobriety.

DIRECTIONS: ▶

Most members of the support group have completed a treatment program of some sort. Upon graduation from the program, most likely the student met with her parents, counselors, and other caregivers who were involved to discuss a plan that will help ensure the student is successful in her recovery. This meeting is often referred to as an exit conference.

In turn, ask group members to share with the rest of the group what their recommended recovery plans are. Use the questions below as a discussion guide.

QUESTIONS: ▶
- Are you following your recommended recovery plan? If not, why?
- Does your recovery plan help you stay clean and sober? How?
- After listening to other group members' recovery plans, is there something about your plan that you would like to change? What is it?

NOTES: ▶

If there are group members who didn't have a recovery plan recommended to them, ask the rest of the group to prescribe a plan for them.

MATERIALS: ▶

None required.

61
Relapse Warning Signs

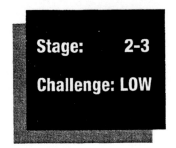

Stage: 2-3

Challenge: LOW

GOALS: ▶
- Identify common relapse warning signs
- Help students identify their own relapse warning signs

DESCRIPTION: ▶ Students examine common relapse warning signs, choosing and discussing those that apply to themselves.

DIRECTIONS: ▶ After first making certain that everyone understands what relapse is and what warning signs refer to, pass out copies of the **Relapse Warning Signs** worksheet (see following page).

When everyone has finished the worksheet, discuss their answers by asking them to tell the rest of the group what their personal warning signs are.

QUESTIONS: ▶
- What are your three most critical relapse warning signs?
- Have you experienced these warning signs before? When?
- What should you do when you are experiencing these warning signs?
- How can the rest of your support group help when you're experiencing these warning signs?

MATERIALS: ▶ **Relapse Warning Signs** worksheet.

Relapse Warning Signs

The road to relapse has plenty of warning signs. If you can recognize these signs, you can turn back *before* you relapse. Here's a list of what happens to people when they are getting dangerously close to using alcohol and other drugs once again. Place a check mark by all the signs that apply to you.

- Stuffing feelings (not talking about your feelings)
- Blowing up (yelling, frustrated over small problems)
- Negative attitude (being critical and judgmental)
- Bored (thinking there's nothing for you to do)
- Self-pity (feeling upset because you can't drink or get high)
- Denial of drug problem (thinking you can control it)
- Aggressive thoughts (thinking about hurting yourself or others)
- Thinking often about using alcohol and other drugs
- Isolation (avoiding family and supportive friends)
- Blaming (thinking everybody else is to blame for your problems)
- Dishonesty (telling lies to cover for yourself)
- School or work troubles (skipping class, flunking, missing work)
- Legal troubles (problems with police or probation officer)
- Conflicts with family members
- Rejecting advice (won't consider suggestions from others)
- Poor meeting attendance (skipping A.A., N.A., or support group)
- Hanging around places where you used to get high or drink
- Spending time with friends you used to drink or get high with

If I were close to relapsing, here's how people could tell:

1)

2)

3)

62
Recovery Curve

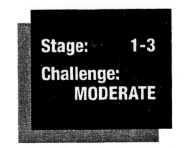

GOALS: ▶

- Clarify personal reasons for staying clean and sober
- Demonstrate how students' lives have improved since abstaining from alcohol and other drugs

DESCRIPTION: ▶

Students describe their progression into chemical dependence and their climb back up in recovery using a time line shaped as a valley.

DIRECTIONS: ▶

Hand out large sheets of newsprint and markers to group members and ask them to draw a line that curves down and then back up, like a valley (see following page for an illustration). Ask them to first describe their progression down the valley into chemical dependence by outlining consequences they've experienced, incidents that showed that their chemical use was getting worse, negative feelings, and behaviors. The bottom of the valley should represent their lives and problem with alcohol and other drugs at its worst.

Then, on the uphill side of the curve, they should describe the progression of their recovery, such as going to treatment, joining a twelve-step group, regaining the trust of family members, feeling better about themselves, celebrating three months of sobriety. The final entry on the curve should represent their present circumstances.

When everyone has finished drawing their recovery curves, spend the remaining time in this session discussing their drawings. You may wish to reserve an entire group session for them to explain their curves to the rest of the group.

MATERIALS: ▶

Newsprint and markers.

RECOVERY CURVE EXAMPLE

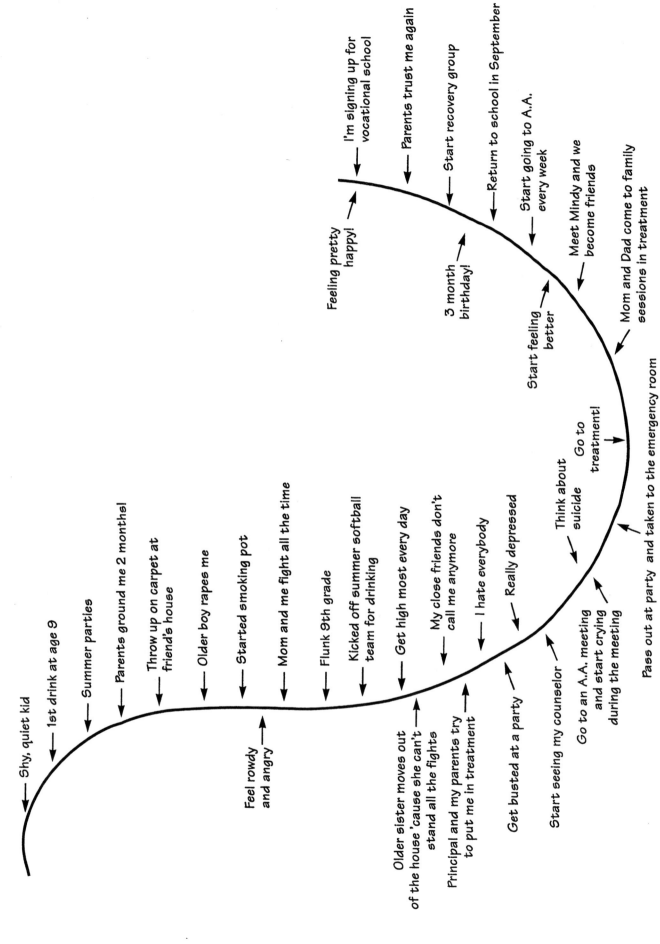

- Shy, quiet kid
- 1st drink at age 9
- Summer parties
- Parents ground me 2 months!
- Throw up on carpet at friend's house
- Older boy rapes me
- Started smoking pot
- Mom and me fight all the time
- Flunk 9th grade
- Feel rowdy and angry
- Kicked off summer softball team for drinking
- Get high most every day
- My close friends don't call me anymore
- I hate everybody
- Really depressed
- Think about suicide
- Go to treatment!
- Older sister moves out of the house 'cause she can't stand all the fights
- Principal and my parents try to put me in treatment
- Get busted at a party
- Start seeing my counselor
- Go to an A.A. meeting and start crying during the meeting
- Pass out at party and taken to the emergency room
- I'm signing up for vocational school
- Parents trust me again
- Start recovery group
- Return to school in September
- Start going to A.A. every week
- Meet Mindy and we become friends
- Mom and Dad come to family sessions in treatment
- Feeling pretty happy!
- 3 month birthday!
- Start feeling better

63
My Danger Zones

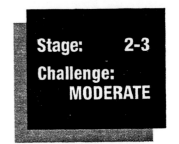
GOALS: ▶

- Help students recognize situations that present risk for a relapse
- Identify solutions for these high-risk situations

DESCRIPTION: ▶

After explaining the concept of danger zones, the group room is set up to demonstrate a continuum ranging from dangerous to safe behaviors pertaining to sobriety. Students use this continuum to assign the degree of risk to a variety of behaviors and situations.

DIRECTIONS: ▶

Begin this session by discussing the concept of danger zones (see **For Your Information** on following page). When everyone understands what danger zones are, label one end of the room as getting high or drunk and the other as perfect sobriety. Point out to the group that the middle of the room represents different degrees of the danger zone. Ask a group member for an example of a situation, feeling, or behavior that would be in her danger zone, such as hanging out with people who are getting stoned. Ask everyone to indicate how risky this experience would be for them personally by standing somewhere between the two ends of the room.

Once everyone is standing still, discuss the variety of positions. One person might be standing over near the sobriety end of the continuum, reporting that the reality is most all his friends drink and he's just had to learn how to live with it; others might be standing very near to the other end, emphatically saying that they can't handle being around people who are actually getting high right in front of them. Encourage frank discussion of these disagreements.

After these differing opinions are discussed, ask the group to talk about how they can reduce the risk of those danger zone situations they can't avoid. For example, the group agrees that they all must come to school, and that school itself can be a danger zone because of the exposure to old friends who are using lots of drugs. So how do they handle this? They might decide that this support group helps and that they can informally spend time together during the day, like during lunch, in the commons, or in study hall.

Continue this activity by asking another group member to select a different danger zone example.

MATERIALS: ▶

None required.

For Your Information . . .

DANGER ZONES

If alcohol and other drug problems were like a big open field, one side would be sobriety, and the other side would be getting high or drunk. When a student is at one end or the other, she—and most likely you—know it; but, when she's somewhere in the middle, it's hard for her to decide in which side of the field she's standing. This middle ground is a danger zone for people staying clean and sober. Group members' danger zone includes those people, places, and activities that increase the chances they'll drink or get high. This danger zone might include a certain friend who always gave them drugs, going to a party where everybody will be getting drunk, or whenever group members' parents leave town for the weekend. It's important for them to understand their danger zone so they can stay out of there whenever possible, and not drink or get high in those danger zone situations they can't avoid.

There are many ways they can deal with their danger zone. The best way is to avoid their danger zone altogether. They can avoid parties where everybody will be drinking and spend little time with old friends who are still getting high.

Unfortunately, there will be some situations they won't be able to avoid. In these situations they need a plan to follow so they won't drink or get high. For example, if a group member is going to his sister's wedding reception, and he knows there will be many people drinking, he could invite a friend who doesn't drink to come along with him. He could make sure there will be nonalcoholic drinks available, or bring his own. Or he could leave the reception early. There are always alternatives. The trick is to be ready, to make a plan beforehand.

64
Relapse Action Plan

GOALS: ▶
- Teach students how to manage urges to use alcohol or other drugs
- Identify activities that help students resist urges to use alcohol or other drugs

DESCRIPTION: ▶ Students are taught a technique for coping successfully with urges to drink or get high.

DIRECTIONS: ▶ Before beginning this activity you'll need to prepare enough Slip Stopper cards for each member of the support group. Copy the card example on the following page onto heavy card stock so that group members can keep these cards in their wallets or purses. You may wish to laminate the cards once they have written on them. These steps ensure a professional-looking card that group members are more likely to take seriously and use when feeling an urge to drink or get high.

Ask group members to share an experience when they wanted to get high or drink. Ask them to describe this urge and how it felt. Oftentimes, group members will report that they felt like "I was going crazy," "I just had to have it," or "I could feel my body just crying out 'Let's go get stoned!'"

Point out to them that, with the exception of a craving brought about by withdrawal from true physical addition, all of this is in their heads. And because it's in their minds, they don't have to act on the urges, no matter how strong, if they don't want to. Some of them might be skeptical at this point, so acknowledge that it is tough to beat these urges, but that it'll be much easier if they use the trick you are going to teach them.

Pass out the **Slip Stopper Plan** and give them a few minutes to complete it (see following page). When they're finished, go around the circle and review everyone's answers. It's important that the group members' answers on the worksheet are practical—that the people listed they could call are really people that group members can get a hold of when necessary, and that the activities listed are realistic and available. Once the worksheets have been discussed, hand out slip stopper cards and ask them to transfer the information onto the cards.

Now explain to them how to use the cards. When they get the urge to get high or drink, here is what they should do:

1. Call someone on your list. If there's no answer, call the next person on the list. When you reach someone, explain that you are thinking about drinking or getting high. Choose one of the activities from your list and tell your friend that instead of using, you're going to do this activity, and that when you're finished you will call again.
2. Begin an activity from your list. If you can't start any of these, choose something else. What's important is that you *do* something—anything but sitting there and thinking about using!
3. After you have finished the activity, and the urge has passed, call your friend again to explain to them how you're feeling.

You may wish to ask group members to practice using these slip stopper cards so they'll be prepared when they're struggling with a strong urge to use. Ask them to practice by pretending, sometime before the next group session, that they're feeling the urge to get high or drunk. Right away they should follow through with the three steps of the plan. As with a fire drill, they should pretend this is the real thing. Spend part of the next group session discussing their experiences with this plan.

MATERIALS: ▶ **Slip Stopper Plan** and Slip Stopper cards.

Slip Stopper Plan

Sometimes people think something is wrong when they get an urge to drink or get high. This is normal during the first year of recovery. After all, you once were drinking and getting high often and a variety of feelings, places, or memories can trigger the urge to use alcohol and other drugs again. It's important to have a sure-fire plan for dealing with these urges when they pop up. Without a plan, you might relapse, especially if the urge comes when you're having a bad day. Three people I can call if I get the urge to drink or get high:

1)

2)

3)

Three activities I can do to get my mind off drinking or getting high:

1)

2)

3)

 -

Slip Stopper Plan Instructions

1. Make the phone call. NOW.
2. Tell your friend you have an urge to use and that, instead, you will (*choose activity*) and will call again when finished.
3. Do the activity.
4. Make the follow-up call.

Name	Phone Number

Instead of using I will:

_____

_____

_____

65
Do's and Don'ts for Sobriety

GOALS: ▶
- Identify attitudes, feelings, and behaviors that will help students remain clean and sober
- Create a list that students can keep for future reference

DESCRIPTION: ▶ Students create a list of things they should and shouldn't do in order to stay clean and sober and take copies of this list home with them.

DIRECTIONS: ▶ Ask group members to make a list on the blackboard of all the things they shouldn't do in order to have a successful recovery from chemical dependence. Once this list is complete, ask them to make another list, this time of all the things they should do to stay clean and sober. As they make them, ask them to keep the lists realistic. For example, perhaps it would be a good idea to go to an A.A. meeting every night, but how many of them would do this?

Once both lists are complete (see following page for an example), the group should review the lists and make any corrections they would like. Ask for two volunteers: one to write the finished lists on a piece of paper, and another to type up the lists. Later in the week, after the typing is finished, make copies for all group members to have. Encourage them to put these lists in places where they will see them frequently, such as taped to the inside of their school locker, on their bedroom door, or on the dashboard of their car.

MATERIALS: ▶ Paper.

Do's and Don'ts for Sobriety List

DO

1. Go to a regular twelve-step meeting.

2. Talk about your feelings.

3. Get involved in positive activities.

4. Spend time connecting with healthy friends.

5. Get enough sleep.

6. Eat right.

7. Try to rebuild relationships with your parents.

8. Spend time being good to yourself.

DON'T

1. Hang around friends who are still drinking or getting high.

2. Go to parties where there will be lots of drinking.

3. Fall back into old behaviors, like skipping school.

4. Sit at home bored.

5. Skip aftercare or your support group.

6. Do things that you need to be dishonest about.

7. Drink or get high.

8. Overdo it (there's only so much you can get done in a day).

66
Summer Vacation Plans

GOALS: ▶
- Identify possible problems concerning remaining sober during summer vacation
- Encourage students to make a recovery plan for their summer vacation

DESCRIPTION: ▶
Students identify possible threats to their sobriety that can occur during summer vacation and make a plan to help ensure their continued abstinence from alcohol and other drugs.

DIRECTIONS: ▶
Ask the group to think about the possible problems that may arise over summer vacation, such as not having a regular support group meeting, loss of contact with recovering peers, or more frequent drinking parties. After this has been discussed, pass out pieces of paper and ask group members to make a plan for their own summer vacation by writing down what they'll do in order to take care of themselves and stay clean and sober. Typical examples could include going to extra twelve-step meetings, spending regular time with a recovering friend, getting a job.

After they've finished their lists, go around the circle and ask group members to tell the rest of the group what their summer plan entails. When someone has finished his list, encourage the rest of the group to tell him whether or not they think this is an adequate plan. After everyone has shared their lists, ask group members if there is anything they want to change in their plan after hearing other group members' plans.

MATERIALS: ▶
Paper.

67
Surviving a Slip

GOALS:

■ Help students prepare for the possibility of a relapse episode
■ Discuss what students should do if they were to relapse

DESCRIPTION: ▶

Students discuss what steps they should take if they were to use alcohol or other drugs.

DIRECTIONS: ▶

Begin this session by encouraging the group to visualize the aftermath of a relapse episode. Ask them to get comfortable, close their eyes and relax by taking ten deeps breaths, each breath slower than the previous one. Once they are relaxed, ask them to imagine waking up after getting very drunk or high at a party the night before. Ask them to concentrate on how they might be feeling. Now ask them to think about what they're going to do once they get up: Tell their parents and counselors? Go get stoned again? Call their sponsor? After giving them a few minutes to consider all of this, ask them to open their eyes and rejoin the group circle.

Begin a discussion by asking group members to share the feelings associated with the relapse—perhaps guilt, remorse, anger, fear—and then what action they took that day. Because group members will have differing opinions concerning what steps should be taken after a relapse, encourage the group to make a list on the blackboard outlining what they should do if they were to relapse. Also use information from the following page to supplement the group's list. Finish this session by asking group members to tell the group, after looking over the list on the blackboard, what steps they'll take if they were ever to relapse.

MATERIALS:

None required.

For Your Information . . .

What Should Recovering Students Do If They Relapse?
Even though it might feel like it to group members (or you), drinking or getting high isn't the end of their world. But a great deal depends on what they do next. Like an ice skater who slips while performing, a recovering teenager can either get up and carry on, or he can stay down and turn a slip into a full relapse. It's a good idea for them to have an emergency plan to follow if they are to drink or get high. This isn't to say that they're going to use, but, like an emergency plan for a house fire, it's a good idea to be prepared just in case. Here are the steps group members should take if they use alcohol or other drugs:

1. Make a commitment
Right away, they must make a commitment to themselves that, regardless of how they feel, they'll stay clean and sober for the next 24 hours. After slipping, they might feel like giving up completely, so this step is important.

2. Be honest
It's vitally important that they tell people they have slipped. There might be someone they won't want to tell—maybe they have a parent who is drinking heavily and won't understand—but, at the very least, they should tell their twelve-step group, sponsor, friends, and you. They'll need the support these people can offer, and if they don't tell them about the slip, these people can't help. **If they aren't honest at this point, the slip will most likely turn into a full relapse!**

3. Learn from their mistake
So, what exactly went wrong? They need to know. A slip is a warning light indicating a problem. They should ask their family, friends, fellow group members, and sponsor what these people think they should do differently.

4. Make the change
Once they understand what went wrong, they should change it. Going to more twelve-step meetings, talking about their feelings more often, staying out of their danger zone—whatever is wrong, they need to fix it. It's easy for them to feel discouraged after a slip, but many young people have relapsed and were able to pick themselves up and carry on. They can too.

Section E:
Support Systems Activities

Completing a treatment program isn't the end of a young person's chemical dependence—it's the beginning of recovery. From this point on, she will need to be a part of a school support group, attend a regular twelve-step group, an aftercare program, and perhaps family or individual counseling.

All of this involves reaching out to others for help, building bridges instead of fences. Though they know this—probably a hundred times they are told "go to meetings, get a sponsor, talk about your feelings," it's easy for group members to, little by little, develop bad habits: avoiding talking about feelings, skipping meetings, spending too much time alone.

While some of this might stem from laziness or unhealthy attitudes, much of group members' resistance to reaching out is simply that they don't know how. The activities in this section focus on evaluating group members' support systems, incorporating the Twelve Steps into their recovery program, and how to ask for help. Twelve-step groups are emphasized because experience shows that these groups are the best resource recovering people have. It's especially helpful for you, as a group leader, to have a practical understanding of these programs, such as Alcoholics Anonymous (A.A.), Narcotics Anonymous (N.A.), and Alateen. Fortunately, this understanding is very simple to come by. Obtain a schedule of the meetings in your community and attend an *open* meeting (open meetings are open to the public, while closed meetings are for anyone with a drinking problem, in the case of A.A.).

With this practical background, a familiarity with the treatment centers and other resources in your community, and these activities, you'll be able to respond appropriately when group members begin isolating themselves or skipping meetings, losing precious ground in the work of recovering from chemical dependence.

68
The Twelve Steps

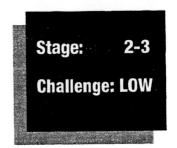

GOALS: ▶
- Help students understand the Twelve Steps
- Encourage students to use the Twelve Steps to help them abstain from chemicals

DESCRIPTION: ▶

Using lecture and examples, students learn how the Twelve Steps can help people with drinking or other drug problems.

DIRECTIONS: ▶

Begin this session by giving group members copies of the **Twelve Steps for Young People** handout and making a brief presentation explaining these Twelve Steps (see following pages and Appendix B). After this introduction, ask group members to create a fictitious young person, whom we'll call Jack, with a chemical dependence problem. The group should set the stage by describing various aspects of Jack's chemical dependence problem, such as use patterns, effects on peer relations, school performance, family tension, and so on. It can be helpful to make notes on the blackboard. Someone may even wish to draw Jack himself on the blackboard. Once Jack has been described, assign the various Steps to group members by numbering off around the circle until all Twelve Steps have been assigned (it's okay if some group members have been assigned more than one Step).

Now tell the group they're going to help Jack stay sober by helping him work the Steps. Each group member should think about how Jack would use his or her assigned step to help himself stay sober. After giving them a few minutes to think about this, ask the group member assigned the first step to describe Jack working this step. For example, "Jack still sometimes has a difficult time admitting he has a drinking problem. When he struggles with this, it puts him in a risky frame of mind for drinking or getting high. So, when he's feeling this way, he stops and thinks about how bad things were and how out of control his life was when he was using chemicals." Continue this process with the remaining steps.

Finish this session by asking group members to discuss how the Twelve Steps help them stay clean and sober.

QUESTIONS: ▶
- Which step is easiest for you to do? Why?
- Which step is most difficult for you? Why?
- Is working these steps helpful for you? How?

NOTES: ▶

If you predict the group will find this task difficult, you may wish to volunteer to describe Jack's work with the first step yourself in order to model desired behavior. The young people's version of the Twelve Steps has been included for younger students, or for those who aren't already familiar with the steps. When the group is composed primarily of students already familiar with the Twelve Steps (which is hopefully the case), you may wish to use the original version (see appendix B).

MATERIALS: ▶

Twelve Steps for Young People handout.

Twelve Steps for Young People

1. I tried to be in charge of my life, but it got messed up.

2. I start trusting a higher power and other people in my life.

3. I reach out and ask for help.

4. I make a list of mistakes I've made.

5. I share my list with someone I really trust.

6. I decide I really do want things to be different for me.

7. I let my higher power and other people help me.

8. I make a list of people whom I've hurt.

9. I apologize to these people and make things right.

10. I work to correct the mistakes that I make.

11. I continue to ask my higher power for help.

12. I share my experiences with others.

For Your Information . . .

The Twelve Steps*

The Twelve Steps are the historical and practical foundation of Alcoholics Anonymous and have since been modified for use in many other self-help groups, such as Al-Anon, Narcotics Anonymous, Gamblers Anonymous, Overeaters Anonymous. Regardless of the program, though, the Twelve Steps remain the same with the exception of what the group feels powerless over in the First Step. In Alcoholics Anonymous the First Step goes like this: "We admitted that we were powerless over alcohol—that our lives had become unmanageable."

The steps are the backbone of all twelve-step programs; members find their sobriety in the steps and continue to return to them as they work on themselves. No one is finished with the steps when reaching number twelve—she continues to practice them in her life.

The first three steps are about surrendering. Simply put, newcomers admit they have a problem, they see there is help available, and they ask for that help. It's the classic ending and beginning for a chemically dependent person: the end of the drinking or getting high, and the beginning of sobriety and a new life.

Steps four through six encourage self-assessment. People beginning to work these steps usually have left a long trail of strained relationships, school troubles, legal disputes, and personal guilt and shame. Their lives are a mess. Now it's time to begin sorting this out by making a list, coming clean by talking about the "secrets" with someone (this person might be a member of the clergy, a counselor, or a friend), and then being willing to leave all this heartache and tragedy behind and start anew.

Steps seven through nine recognize that chemically dependent people need to live in community with others. It's important that they be willing to reach out and ask for help, to take a good long look at the people they've hurt, and then to make amends.

The last three steps involve action. They become an integral part of what twelve-step group members refer to as their "Program." They continue to correct any mistakes they make, they look for direction and guidance in their sobriety, and they help other struggling chemically dependent people find sobriety by reminding themselves that "We keep what we have by giving it away."

---

*For additional information on the Twelve Steps and twelve-step groups in general, see Appendix B and the Resources section.

69 Visiting a Twelve-step Meeting

GOALS: ▶
- Increase awareness of community resources
- Encourage students to begin attending Twelve-step groups

DESCRIPTION: ▶

Students visit an Alcoholics Anonymous or Narcotics Anonymous meeting and discuss their experiences the following group session.

DIRECTIONS: ▶

First, you'll need to obtain a copy of the twelve-step meeting schedule for your community. It will also be helpful to find out which meetings would be best for young people to attend, as meetings have personalities all their own. If there are group members who are already attending meetings, this might be a good choice for the other group members.

After everyone knows where the meetings are, ask them all to choose and attend an A.A. or N.A. meeting. They may wish to go together as a large group, or less formally in several smaller groupings. If there are members currently attending meetings, perhaps they could help new group members get to a meeting. The following week, ask group members to discuss their impressions and experiences.

QUESTIONS: ▶
- How were you feeling when you first entered the meeting room? And afterwords?
- What did the speakers have in common?
- What did you have in common with the speakers?
- What was the mood in the meeting room?
- What did you hear during the meeting that was helpful for you?
- DId you hear anything during the meeting that you disagreed with?
- How would you describe this meeting?
- Would this meeting be helpful for you?

NOTES: ▶

Group members usually don't like this assignment. Often this reaction stems from fear concerning a new and unknown situation. Encouraging them to go together reduces this uneasiness. However they get there, it's crucial that these students start attending twelve-step meetings to ensure their continued sobriety. Some recovery support groups make regular twelve-step meeting attendance mandatory.

MATERIALS: ▶

Twelve-step meeting schedules.

70
Twelve-step Support

GOALS: ▶
- Increase awareness of community resources
- Encourage students to begin attending Twelve-step groups

DESCRIPTION: ▶ Students are introduced to twelve-step groups of Alcoholics Anonymous and Narcotics Anonymous through guest speakers and literature.

DIRECTIONS: ▶ Arrange for a member of a local Alcoholics Anonymous or Narcotics Anonymous group to come and speak to your support group. To do so, call the contact number listed in your phone book and ask for a public speaker.

It's a good idea to discuss this topic the week previous to the speaker's presentation. Ask group members if they have had any experience with twelve-step groups before. What are their perceptions about these programs? Ask them to explain, in their own words, what purpose these groups serve. Encourage debate as this tension will stimulate questions and interest in the speaker the following week. Appoint a member of the group to record the disagreements and questions brought up during this discussion. All of this can then be raised to the speaker.

NOTES: ▶ When requesting a speaker, ask for someone whom your group members can readily relate to—a young recovering person who abused street drugs instead of an older person whose chemical experience was limited to alcohol. Limit this speaker's presentation so there will be time for questions and discussion.

MATERIALS: ▶ None required.

71
Step Study

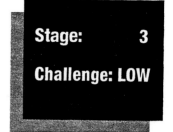

GOALS: ▶
- Help students understand the Twelve Steps
- Encourage students to use the Twelve Steps to help them abstain from chemicals

DESCRIPTION: ▶

Students study the Twelve Steps of Alcoholics Anonymous and discuss how they can apply them to their lives.

DIRECTIONS: ▶

There are several possible ways to approach this activity. Since it's impossible to discuss all twelve of the steps in any detail during a single session of group, it's best to split up the discussion into many parts. You may wish to focus on a single step each week or perhaps make the last session of each month be designated "step study week."

When designating an entire session to study one of the steps, first read the particular step out loud and then ask each group member to describe what the step means to her and how she applies it in her life. If the group is going to study one of the steps for only a part of the group session, choose only one person to read the step and explain what it means to him and how he applies it to his life. When using this approach, it can be helpful to assign the steps in advance so group members will be ready when it's their turn to present.

NOTES: ▶

There is a wealth of literature available that will help group members understand the Twelve Steps. One resource in particular you may wish to use is the *Twelve Steps and Twelve Traditions* (see Resources section).

MATERIALS: ▶

None required.

72
The Importance of a Sponsor

GOALS:
- Help students understand why they need a sponsor
- Teach students how to find an appropriate sponsor

DESCRIPTION:

Students learn what a sponsor is, why they need one, and how to get one through group discussion.

DIRECTIONS:

Going around the circle, ask group members if they have a sponsor. If they do, ask them to tell the group how they got this sponsor, how he or she helps them stay sober, and how they take good care of themselves. For those who don't have a sponsor, ask them—without shaming them—to explain why not. If there are group members who don't know what a sponsor is, ask the rest of the group to explain.

Assuming that there'll be some group members who either don't have a sponsor or don't like the sponsor they now have, pass out copies of the **Choosing a Sponsor** worksheet (see following page). After they've completed the bottom section, ask those members of the group who don't have a sponsor if they are now going to ask someone to be their sponsor. You may wish to ask them to commit themselves to a specific date—in other words, "I'll have asked someone to be my sponsor by the next time our group meets."

NOTES:

A group member must be going to twelve-step meetings before he can get a sponsor because sponsorship is an integral part of twelve-step programs.

MATERIALS:

Choosing a Sponsor worksheet.

Choosing a Sponsor

A sponsor is an important part of a Recovery Program. This person is a member of a twelve-step meeting who can serve as a counselor, big brother or sister, and friend all rolled into one. Use this list to help you choose a sponsor. If you already have a sponsor, look over this list to see if he or she has some of these qualitites. If not, there's nothing wrong with finding a new sponsor.

Qualities of a good sponsor include:

Strong Sobriety. Your sponsor needs at least two years of sobriety and should be working a good recovery program.

Role Model. Your sponsor should be someone who acts and talks in ways you admire. This person should have qualities you also want.

Same Sex. Your sponsor should be the same gender as you.

Trustworthy. You need a sponsor who you trust will keep what you share confidential.

Reliable. Your sponsor needs to be available to help when you need help.

Honesty. You need a sponsor who will be honest with you, even if it means telling you things you don't want to hear.

Three people who would be a good sponsor for me:

Name	Qualities this person has to offer
1)	1)
2)	2)
3)	3)

73
Dear Andy

GOALS: ▶
- Find solutions for problems common to students recovering from chemical dependence
- Learn new coping skills

DESCRIPTION: ▶

Group members read fictitious letters to an advice columnist and discuss solutions to the problems raised in these letters.

DIRECTIONS: ▶

Taking turns, students should choose and then read aloud a letter from the samples provided (see following page). After reading the letter, the group should discuss what advice it would give.

MATERIALS: ▶

Sample letters.

Dear Andy Letters

Dear Andy:
My dad has a drinking problem. He doesn't live with us anymore. Since he's left, my mom is always too busy or tired to pay any attention to me. Instead she's always worrying about the bills and is sad or crabby most of the time. I feel like my dad forgot all about me and that I'm just one more problem for my mom. Now things have gotten bad at school 'cause I just don't care about homework or grades any more. My mom and me fight all the time and I feel angry, lonely, and confused.

John

Dear Andy:
I'm getting out of treatment in a week. My problem is my family. My Mom's got a real bad drinking problem, and most of my family refused to even come visit me here in the treatment center. In other words, I won't get any support at home for staying straight. My counselor wants me to go live in a halfway house here in town, but I want to live at home. Even though it'll be tough, I think I can make it. What should I do?

Sonny

Dear Andy:
My younger brother has a bad drug problem. Whenever our parents are gone, he's off in his room getting high or inviting friends over to party. A few days ago, he stole some liquor from our parents. Dad saw that it was gone and started accusing all of us kids, especially me since he knows I used to drink a lot. Now he's demanding someone confess. My brother told me that if I say anything, he'll never speak to me again. I don't want to narc on my brother, but I don't want to be blamed, either.

Sandra

Dear Andy:
I met this girl in my aftercare group and we've started going out together. At first I thought she was staying sober—I mean that's what she's telling everybody in group—but now I've found out that she's really drinking at parties and lying to all of us. I really like her and want to keep seeing her but, at the aftercare sessions, I feel like I've got to cover up for her and her drinking. If I blow the whistle on her, I'm sure she'll dump me; on the other hand, I hate being dishonest to my friends in the group.

Manuel

Dear Andy:
Last summer I quit drinking, and I've been doing great. This fall, though, I joined the basketball team and the rest of the team does a lot of partying. I hang around with them and it's getting harder and harder to resist getting drunk right along with them. I don't want to lose them as friends, but I don't want to blow my sobriety either.

Melanie

74
Asking for Help

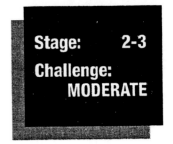

GOALS: ▶
- Encourage students to take care of themselves
- Teach them how to reach out effectively for assistance

DESCRIPTION: ▶
Students discuss the types of support available to themselves and use role plays to practice asking for the support they need.

DIRECTIONS: ▶
Ask the group to list all the different types of support available to them, such as friends, parents, twelve-step meetings, school counselors, support groups, crisis phone lines. Give group members three small pieces of paper and ask them to briefly describe three problems, one on each piece of paper. These problems can be situations they've experienced personally or that would be typical for someone in their group, such as feeling like they want to get high, worried that they're pregnant, family problems, or flunking a class in school.

Once finished, collect the papers and mix them up. Ask someone to draw a slip of paper and read it out loud to the group. Everyone should then review the list of possible support options and decide which one would be best for this specific problem. For example, a student is upset because her boyfriend has started hitting her when he's angry and she doesn't know what to do about it. The group thinks that in this situation the best thing to do would be to talk with the school counselor about it as a first step.

Once the group has made this decision, this first step should be role-played. The student who drew the slip of paper should be the one asking for help, so let her choose another group member to play the school counselor. Once the roles and the issue are clear, encourage the two students to role-play the first meeting when the student approaches the counselor for help. Ask them to do this either in the center of the circle or in front of the room. You may wish to set up a few props to add more realism to the role play. Once they are finished, ask a different group member to draw a new slip of paper.

NOTES: ▶
The role plays should focus only on the initial asking of help, not the resolution of the problem. The goal of this activity is to help group members learn how to reach out and ask for help in a variety of situations.

MATERIALS: ▶
Paper, props if desired.

75
My Support System

GOALS: ▶
- Encourage students to evaluate their support systems
- Identify other available support options

DESCRIPTION: ▶
Students identify what they use for personal support in their recovery program and consider other means of getting support.

DIRECTIONS: ▶
Ask the group to define what a support system is to them, such as "all the people, places, and things that help you stay sober and take good care of yourself." After everyone understands what a support system is, pass out copies of **My Support System** worksheet (see following page).

When everyone is finished, ask group members to share their answers with the rest of the group. Once everyone has done this, start around the circle again, but this time ask the rest of the group to give the person whose turn it is some feedback about her support system. The questions below can be used as a guideline for this part of the activity.

QUESTIONS: ▶
- What's involved in your support system?
- How does your support system help you?
- What does your support system lack?
- What could you add to your support system?
- How is your support system different from that of other group members?

MATERIALS: ▶
My Support System worksheet.

My Support System

Consider your support system. Who are the people that help you stay clean and sober? For everything that helps you stay sober—friends, teachers, parents, twelve-step groups, girlfriends, boyfriends, support groups, counselors, a Higher Power—add a leg of support to the drawing. Be sure to write the people's names on the legs also. One leg has already been drawn to get you started.

76
Down in the Dumps

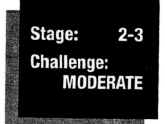
GOALS: ▶
- Help students cope with depressing feelings
- Teach students the symptoms of depression

DESCRIPTION: ▶

Students learn how to cope with depressing feelings through discussion and a checklist. The symptoms of serious depression are also discussed.

DIRECTIONS: ▶

Begin this session by asking students what depression is, and how you can tell if you're depressed. Then ask group members to share personal examples of when they've felt down or depressed. Also ask them to tell the group what they did to deal with those feelings. Ask the group if anyone is currently struggling with blue feelings or depression. Ask them to describe this in more detail. Pass out copies of the **Down in the Dumps** checklist to everyone.

NOTES: ▶

If there's a member of the group who seems to be seriously depressed, it would be helpful to talk with this student about this and possibly to make a referral to a school or community counselor for evaluation. There is a strong relationship between relapse and depression.

MATERIALS: ▶

Down in the Dumps checklist.

Down in the Dumps Checklist

When you're feeling sad, blue, or depressed, it's tough to shake it off and tell yourself to cheer up. It's even worse when other people tell you this. So what do you do—stay depressed forever? Hardly. Mild depression and that down-in-the-dumps feeling usually just go away after a while. But in the meantime here are some things that you can do to help yourself feel better right now:

1. **Make yourself a schedule every morning and stick to it**. For example, "I'm going to school today; seventh period I'm going to get my project done in the art room; after school I'm going to go over to Kurt's house; tonight, I'm going to go to A.A."

2. **Get physical!** Mowing the lawn, running, shooting hoops—these kind of activities often help you burn off frustration and negative energy.

3. **Only eight hours of sleep**. Spending all day in bed will only make you feel worse.

4. **Eat regular meals.** Even if you're not hungry, eat anyway.

5. **Make a feel-good list.** Take a moment when you're not feeling depressed to write down a list of things that help you feel good, like going to a movie, playing your guitar, going out for pizza with a bunch of friends. Make this list at least ten items long. When you're feeling depressed, look at your list, pick something from it, and do it. Simple, huh?

77
Enabling

GOALS: ▶
- Help students identify enabling behaviors
- Motivate students to stop enabling friends and family

DESCRIPTION: ▶

Students discuss various enabling behaviors they have witnessed and complete an enabling inventory.

DIRECTIONS: ▶

Begin this session with a description of enabling (see **For Your Information** on following pages). It's important that everyone understands not only what enabling is, but also why it's not a good idea.

Ask the group to volunteer examples of enabling they've witnessed, such as a group member hearing his mother call in sick for his father who was really hung over, or a group member who watched a friend give her homework to another student to copy who had been out drinking the previous night. After everyone has given an example, ask group members to share a personal example of when they have enabled a friend or family member.

Now hand out the **Enabling Inventory** worksheet (see following pages). When everyone has finished, discuss their scores. Spend the remaining time in the session making a list of ways group members can avoid enabling other people, such as refusing to lie for a friend, or not making excuses for a parent's drug problem.

MATERIALS: ▶

Enabling Inventory worksheet.

Enabling Inventory

Answer the questions by making a check mark in the appropriate column.

No   Sometimes   Yes

___   ___   ___   1. I'd prefer a friend keep on using chemicals than have him meet with the school counselor.

___   ___   ___   2. I've introduced a friend to chemicals.

___   ___   ___   3. I've been concerned about a friend's chemical use but have been afraid to talk to her about it.

___   ___   ___   4. I've been concerned about a friend's chemical use but haven't talked to a teacher or counselor about it.

___   ___   ___   5. I'm afraid that if I share my concern with a friend I'll lose his friendship.

___   ___   ___   6. I'm afraid others would think I'm a narc and that sharing my concerns about a friend would affect my reputation in school.

___   ___   ___   7. I blame other things or people for a friend's chemical use or problem.

___   ___   ___   8. I've protected and covered up for a friend who has a chemical problem.

___   ___   ___   9. I avoid being around chemical users I'm worried about.

___   ___   ___   10. I'm not able to break up with my boyfriend or girlfriend even though his or her chemical use causes me problems.

Add up your score by giving yourself 1 point for every "sometimes" answer and 2 points for every "yes" answer.

The information in this inventory was adapted from *From Peer Pressure to Peer Support* by Shelley MacKay Freeman (see Resources section).

For Your Information . . .

Enabling

When we do something that's harmful to ourselves or others, we often experience some type of consequence. It's one of the ways that Life teaches us important lessons. People abusing alcohol and other drugs experience many consequences: hangovers, flunked classes, family problems, lost jobs, trouble with the police. You would think that these experiences would help them make changes in their behavior rather quickly. That's not the case, though.

Are these people slow? Stubborn? Not any more so than the rest of us. The reason they don't make changes in their behaviors is because they don't experience the consequences. And the reason they don't experience consequences is because people around them—often family or friends—come to their rescue.

This is called *enabling,* and it's the term used to describe things people do (or don't do, for that matter) that shield a person in trouble with chemicals from experiencing the consequences they really need to feel. The classic example would be the wife calling in sick for her husband who's really just hung over. She does it for obvious reasons: She doesn't want him to lose his job, get upset with her, or be in a worse mood than he already is. But what does the husband now know? Every time he drinks too much in the evening (which is happening more frequently), he knows that his wife will come to the rescue. She wants him to quit drinking, and yet her actions allow him to drink even more. The opposite effect of what she wants!

Enabling is understandable. When we see someone we care about in trouble, we almost automatically come to that person's rescue. But, if we really care about people in trouble with chemicals, we'll allow them to experience the consequences of their actions because it's only after feeling this pain that they will finally say "Ouch!" and make some changes in their behavior.

Here are a few more examples of enabling:

A student letting a friend copy her homework though she knows he didn't get his done because he was out partying all weekend.

A teacher avoiding confronting a student in his class who he thinks might be high.

A principal calling a student in trouble with chemicals into her office and yelling at him to shape up but not getting him any help.

Friends of a chemically dependent student not saying anything about his chemical use because they're afraid he'll get angry.

78
Is My Friend in Trouble?

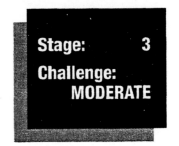

Stage: 3
Challenge:
MODERATE

GOALS: ▶
- Help students determine if friends are in trouble with their own chemical use
- Set the stage for beginning an intervention

DESCRIPTION: ▶

Students complete an assessment instrument that helps them determine if a friend is in trouble with chemicals.

DIRECTIONS: ▶

Ask group members to think of someone close to them whose chemical use concerns them. Going around the circle, ask them to describe this person's chemical use to the group. Typically, group members will have difficulty making a judgment about the severity of the problem. They are uneasy about their friend or family member's chemical use, but they don't really know how to rate the problem.

Hand out the questionnaire on the following pages to the group members. After they have completed it, discuss the results. Ask them if the questionnaire results agree with their own opinions. Spend the remaining group time discussing what actions they could take to express their concerns and help the friend or family member they're concerned about.

NOTES: ▶

Activity #79, **Sharing Your Concerns**, is a natural follow-up for this activity.

MATERIALS: ▶

Is My Friend in Trouble? questionnaire.

Is My Friend in Trouble?

Answer each question by placing a check mark in the "yes" or "no" column. Even if you can answer yes to only one part of a question that has several parts, answer the entire question with a yes.

SECTION I

Yes   No

____ ____ 1. Has this person ever been arrested on a MIP (Minor in Possession charge) or been at a party broken up by the police?

____ ____ 2. Has this person ever been suspended from school activities for using chemicals? Has this person dropped school or other activities that used to be important to him or her?

____ ____ 3. Do most of this person's friends use chemicals?

____ ____ 4. Has this person ever had a hangover or a bad trip because of chemical use?

____ ____ 5. Has this person ever lied to you or made excuses about chemical use?

____ ____ 6. Does this person experience unexplainable mood changes or emotional ups and downs?

____ ____ 7. Has this person ever embarrassed you or other friends because of chemical use?

SECTION II

Yes   No

____ ____ 8. Has this person ever been arrested for shoplifting, vandalism, driving while intoxicated, or possession of alcohol or other drugs?

____ ____ 9. Has this person ever been suspended from school for possession of chemicals or fighting?

____ ____ 10. Has this person stolen money from her house or stolen things that could be sold? Or stolen alcohol?

____ ____ 11. Has this person changed friends from those who don't use chemicals to those who do?

____ ____ 12. Has this person experienced a significant weight loss or gain, unexplained injuries, respiratory problems or overdoses? Has his appearance or personal hygiene become sloppy?

continued on next page

SECTION II CONTINUED . . .

___ ___ 13. Does it appear harder for this person to pay attention to something or someone for a long time? Does she have less motivation than before? Has this person had memory lapses?

___ ___ 14. Have you heard this person saying things like "I wish I were dead"?

___ ___ 15. Does this person strongly defend his right to drink or use other drugs?

___ ___ 16. Have you witnessed this person manipulating her parents to lie or cover up for her at school, at work, or with friends?

SECTION III

___ ___ 17. Has this person ever been arrested for robbery, drug dealing, assault and battery, or prostitution?

___ ___ 18. Has this person been suspended from school more than once, or expelled?

___ ___ 19. Has this person stayed away from home for more than a weekend, or even left home "for good"?

___ ___ 20. Has this person become violent with his friends, or started avoiding them?

___ ___ 21. Has this person experienced obvious weight loss or injuries? Has she ever overdosed, had the shakes, dry heaves, or chronic coughing?

___ ___ 22. Does this person blame her parents, friends, or others for the problems she is experiencing? Does she seem to be angry all the time? Does she have trouble remembering things she said or did?

___ ___ 23. Has this person ever made suicide plans, left suicide notes, or actually attempted suicide?

___ ___ 24. Are you afraid for this person's safety because of any of the behaviors described in this questionnaire?

What your responses mean:

■ "No" answers to most of questions 1 – 7 indicate that this person is probably not involved in chemical use.
■ "Yes" answers to most of questions 1 – 7 indicate that this person is misusing chemicals.
■ "Yes" answers to most of questions 8 – 16 indicate that this person is probably abusing chemicals.
■ "Yes" answers to most of questions 17 – 24 indicate that this person is probably chemically dependent.

The information in this questionnaire was adapted from *Choices & Consequences: What to Do When a Teenager Uses Alcohol/Drugs* by Dick Schaefer (see Resources section).

79
Sharing Your Concerns

GOALS: ▶

- Encourage students to confront their friends who are in trouble
- Teach students how to express themselves in a manner that peers can hear

DESCRIPTION: ▶

Students learn basic confrontation techniques and role-play situations similar to personal concerns.

DIRECTIONS: ▶

Ask group members to think of someone they are close to who is in trouble of some sort. This could be trouble with chemicals, with staying clean and sober, depression, or whatever. On a piece of paper, group members should write three behaviors related to this person that concern them. Go around the circle, asking group members if they've ever told this person their concerns. Most will say "no." Ask them why they haven't shared their concerns and discuss their answers, which typically include "I'm afraid he'd get angry," "It's not really any of my business," "She'd deny it all."

Use this opportunity to teach group members how to communicate their concerns in a manner that will be heard by the friend or family member. Typically, we all share our concerns with statements like this: "You drink too much," or "If you don't start going to A.A., you're going to relapse." Unfortunately, this automatically puts the person on the defensive and leads to arguing and minimizing. Demonstrate this by asking for a volunteer to sit in the center of the circle and pretend to be someone who's in trouble. Then ask everyone to share his or her concerns with this person in the center, pretending this person is the one whom they're concerned about. Expect lots of arguing, defensiveness, and frustration.

There's a better way. The communication framework to use is this: "I feel (name a feeling) when you (describe a behavior)." For example: "I feel sad when I see you staying stoned all the time," "I feel angry when we were supposed to go to a meeting together, and instead you stayed home and watched TV," "I feel scared when you get frustrated and start yelling at Mom." When you communicate something by owning your own feelings it has a powerful effect. How can someone argue with that? They can't tell you that you don't feel that way!

Now ask group members to do the same role play, only this time everyone should phrase their concerns with "I" statements. Afterwards, discuss how much more effective this approach is. Finish this session by asking the group if they are going to approach the friend or family member with their concerns. Follow up on this during the next session of group by asking them how it went.

QUESTIONS: ▶

- Who is the person you are concerned about?
- What is it that concerns you?
- Have you ever tried to share your concerns? What happened?
- Will you be able to share your concerns now using "I" statements?
- Do you think these concerns will be heard?
- Is there anyone else who's also concerned about this person?
- Could you share these concerns together?

NOTES: ▶

If there's someone in the group who isn't concerned about anyone (or at least makes that statement), this person would be a good choice for the center role. If everyone has concerns, either take this role yourself, or have students take turns so that all have a chance to practice "I" statements.

MATERIALS: ▶

Paper.

Section F:
Goals and Decisions Activities

Up until now, group members' lives have been characterized by irresponsibility, unkept promises, poor decisions. They were a mess. While their lives are most likely much more positive now, newly found abstinence from chemicals doesn't necessarily mean they are able to set and work towards personal goals and decisions.

After all, these young people are still teenagers. They are impulsive and have a tough time delaying gratification, especially since they're accustomed to the immediate rewards of a chemical high instead of working towards a lasting sense of satisfaction and achievement.

Though they might not want to hear it, good things really do take time and effort. We can help group members succeed by teaching them how to set goals, make healthy decisions, and recognize and remove their personal stumbling blocks. Clarifying what it is they want out of life, being assertive with peers, abstaining from alcohol and other drugs—the skills group members need in order to achieve their goals—are outlined in this section.

80
Making Choices

GOALS:

■ Learn decision-making technique
■ Practice decision-making process

DESCRIPTION: ▶

Students learn about and then practice healthy decision-making skills using real-life problems.

DIRECTIONS: ▶

Introduce this activity by encouraging group members to describe problems they've had in the past in which they had to decide on a course of action. Examples might include deciding whether to drink alcohol at a party, how to handle an overbearing friend, or what to do about the drinking problem of a family member.

Before handing out the **Making Choices** worksheet (see following page), explain the different steps to the decision-making process, using a situation that you or the group selects and the worksheet as a guide. Once the group understands the different steps, ask them to complete step one of the worksheet.

After everyone has identified a problem that they don't know how to handle, go around the group circle, asking everyone to share the problem they chose in step one. When a group member shares her problem, each member of group should volunteer a possible solution. She can record these solutions in step two. Steps three and four of the worksheet can then be completed individually. When everyone has finished step four, ask group members to share their worksheets. Challenge them to follow through on their chosen course of action sometime before the next group session so that, during the following session, the outcomes can be discussed and the final step of the worksheet can be completed.

MATERIALS:

Making Choices worksheet.

Making Choices

STEP ONE: What is the problem?

STEP TWO: What are your possible choices? (Ask the group.)

1 -

2 -

3 -

4 -

5 -

STEP THREE: Think about your choices.

positive aspects   **negative aspects**

1 -

2 -

3 -

4 -

5 -

STEP FOUR Decide which choice is the best for you.

STEP FIVE Follow through with this choice.

STEP SIX Afterwards, reflect on the choice you made.

Looking back, was this really the best choice?

Will you do anything differently next time you're in this situation?

81
How I Want to Be When I Grow Up

GOALS:

- Encourage students to set personal goals
- Draw attention to the importance of emotional health

DESCRIPTION: ▶

Students describe what kind of people—happy, confident, mature, sensitive—they want to be ten years from now and then discuss what steps need to be taken to ensure this will happen.

DIRECTIONS: ▶

Point out to the group that so often when the future is discussed, we all think in terms of where we want to live or what we want to be doing—"What do you want to be when you grow up?" This activity focuses, instead, on *how* you want to be when you grow up. Do you want to be someone whom others turn to for help? Someone whom little children like? Do you want to be quiet and thoughtful or the life of the party? Do you want to still be struggling with angry feelings all the time, or learn how to let go of them and be more easygoing?

   Ask students to fill out the worksheet (see following page). When everyone is finished, ask them to share their answers with the group. After they have shared both the Now and Future categories, ask group members to describe what is different between the first and second category. Once a student has identified what needs changing (she wants to be more outgoing in the future, for example), ask her what needs to happen for this change to take place. If she isn't able to think of a plan, ask the group for suggestions. For example, a student might, in the future, like to be the kind of person who spends time thinking about what he needs and taking care of himself, and now he sees himself as always worrying about everybody else. The group might suggest to him that every day he do at least one thing for himself rather than going straight home to check whether his dad has been getting high again.

NOTES: ▶

If students don't offer advice and look to you for suggestions, resist. Instead, ask another group member what she thinks this student should do to make these changes.

MATERIALS: ▶

How I Want to Be When I Grow Up worksheet.

How I Want to Be When I Grow Up

Below, list eight examples that describe the kind of person you are now (not *what* you do, but *who* you are and what you are like). Examples could include I'm outgoing, I worry about things too much, I solve everyone's problems, I love to laugh, I'm a good listener.

1)_____

2)_____

3)_____

4)_____

5)_____

6)_____

7)_____

8)_____

Now think about the kind of person you'd like to be ten years from now. Do you want to reduce your shyness and be more outgoing? Do you no longer want to worry so much about what other people think about you? Go ahead and dream. List eight qualities you would like to have be a part of you ten years from now:

1)_____

2)_____

3)_____

4)_____

5)_____

6)_____

7)_____

8)_____

82
Goals and Decisions

Stage: 2-3

Challenge: LOW

GOALS: ▶
- Reinforce personal decisions made by students
- Encourage goal setting
- Identify personal needs and issues

DESCRIPTION: ▶
Group members are asked to identify and set personal goals for themselves and share them with the rest of the group.

DIRECTIONS: ▶
Ask group members to think about the personal issues and problems they have identified as a result of participating in their support group. Pass out sheets of paper and ask them to write these personal issues in the form of a goal that they can work towards. Typical examples include making their sobriety a priority in their lives, talking more about their feelings with friends, or learning more about how the chemical dependence in their family has affected them.

   After everyone has had time to write down their goals and decisions, ask group members to share their answers with the rest of the group. Encourage the rest of the group to give feedback to a student after she has finished sharing her goals and decisions. For example, the group might remind a student about when she told the group she needs to go running when she's feeling angry and is tempted to get high. Then she can add this additional goal to her list.

NOTES: ▶
This activity can be used either in the early stages of group or later on, after students are more aware of their own issues and needs. Using this activity during the initial sessions of group is beneficial in that these clarified goals will provide a sense of direction for the group. You might find, though, that students won't be able to identify personal issues or goals at this early stage. In this case, it will be better to save this activity for later when the students' awareness level has been raised. Or, use this activity twice and compare the goals. Group members might find their personal goals to be quite different the second time around.

MATERIALS: ▶
None required.

83
Stumbling Blocks

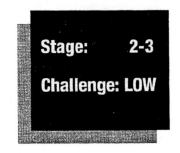

GOALS: ▶
- Help students identify things that interfere with making positive changes
- Discuss methods for solving this interference

DESCRIPTION: ▶
Students identify and discuss those things in their lives that prevent them from making positive changes.

DIRECTIONS: ▶
Begin this session by asking the group to define what is meant by "taking care of yourself." If need be, steer them in the direction of defining this concept as all those things you do that are healthy, positive, and affirming. This includes everything from attending classes to following curfew, talking about their feelings to working the Twelve Steps, staying clean and sober to dealing with stress constructively. Ask group members if they're always successful in taking care of themselves. Of course, the answer to this question will be no. Tell them that you have a worksheet for them to complete that will help them understand what interferes with their ability to be good to themselves (see following page). After everyone has completed the worksheet, spend the remaining time discussing their answers.

QUESTIONS: ▶
- How many of you have similar stumbling blocks?
- What are these common stumbling blocks?
- Have you always had stumbling blocks in your life?
- Why or why not?
- Have you tried to get rid of these stumbling blocks before?
- Were you successful? Why or why not?

MATERIALS: ▶
Stumbling Blocks worksheet.

Stumbling Blocks

For each block below fill in something that interferes with your being able to take care of yourself. These stumbling blocks might include a certain friend, not getting enough sleep, cigarettes, not going to A.A. meetings, a girlfriend, or television, for example.

How I can deal with these stumbling blocks or at least avoid them:

1.

2.

3.

4.

Material for this worksheet adapted from *From Peer Pressure to Peer Support* by Shelley MacKay Freeman (see Resources section).

84
From Now On

Stage: 4

Challenge: LOW

GOALS: ▶
- Encourage goal setting
- Support personal changes made by group members

DESCRIPTION: ▶
Group members review lessons they have learned about themselves during the course of group and identify new behaviors they will continue to practice.

DIRECTIONS: ▶
Review previous sessions of group for the students, pointing out various lessons that have been presented. These examples might include learning that it's important to talk about your feelings, learning how to say no, learning that your sobriety must come first. After reviewing these past lessons, ask them to reflect on the personal lessons they have learned during group. Then hand out the **From Now On** worksheet (see following page). When they have finished, spend the remaining group time sharing their answers.

NOTES: ▶
If there is an important personal lesson that you think a group member failed to remember and record on her worksheet, bring it to her attention. For example: "What about last week, Cindy, when you realized you never have any time to spend alone. Is that something that should be included on your list of things to do from now on?" After meeting with these students for a number of sessions, you probably will have specific concerns about some members of the support group. For example, you might notice that Danny often talks about how he gets upset when his girlfriend has been drinking, or that Betsy spends a lot of time worrying about whether people like her or not. If these students do not address these issues on their worksheets, you can bring it to their attention.

MATERIALS: ▶
From Now On worksheet.

151 / Section F: Goals and Decisions Activities

From Now On

On this worksheet list the things that you will do differently based on what you have learned in your support group.

From now on, I'm going to	Instead of
From now on, I'm going to	Instead of
From now on, I'm going to	Instead of
From now on, I'm going to	Instead of
From now on, I'm going to	Instead of

85
Abstinence Contracts

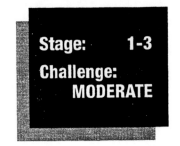

GOALS: ▶
- Encourage students to abstain from chemicals
- Provide constructive consequences for chemical use

DESCRIPTION: ▶

Group members sign abstinence contracts containing consequences that address their specific situations and needs.

DIRECTIONS: ▶

Discuss with group members the importance of their chemical abstinence for the duration of the support group cycle. The foundation of a recovery group is the sobriety of the group members. For some group members, sobriety comes easy; for others, it's a struggle.

This being the case, formally challenge the group to make a commitment to stay abstinent for the duration of the group cycle (even though the group most likely will meet all year, break this challenge down into a smaller time period such as a school quarter or semester). Stress that this abstinence includes all mind-altering chemicals, including alcohol (the exception would be drugs prescribed by a physician). This should be formalized by a written contract (see following page). Ask them to read over the contract and fill in the appropriate blanks. They should do this individually, not as a group, since negative group pressure can easily influence the contents of the contracts. Once group members have completed their contract, collect them and ask group members to tell the group what sort of commitment they made and whether they think this will be an easy or difficult commitment to keep.

NOTES: ▶

Sometimes contracts with consequences invite dishonesty within the group. What happens when someone breaks her contract and is afraid to confess? This should be discussed in the group. It can be helpful to check in—"Did you stay clean and sober this week?"—at the beginning of every session to encourage disclosure of any chemical use.

Also, when nearing the end of the contract period, the group should complete another contract for the following group cycle. It's important to do this before the contract time lapses.

MATERIALS: ▶

Abstinence Contract.

Abstinence Contract

I will not use **any** mind-altering chemicals for the following time period:

_____ to _____.

If I break this commitment, I will take these steps:

1. _____

2. _____

3. _____

And these will be my consequences:

1. _____

2. _____

3. _____

Signed _____ Date _____

Witnessed _____

Section G: Stress Reduction Activities

Stress isn't a problem reserved for adults. Young people experience it too. And their coping styles and ability or inability to deal with stress parallels our own. Taking tests, beginning junior or senior high school, preparing for college, relationship difficulties, family problems, hormonal changes, acute peer pressure, extremely negative self-perceptions, and just figuring out how to grow up are all potential sources of stress. Recovering young people have some extra sources of stressors: struggling to stay sober, returning back to school from a month at a treatment center to find an academic nightmare of failing grades, incomplete work, resentments and doubts expressed by teachers familiar with the student's history, rejection by their drug-using peer group, and deep-seated family troubles.

Now that they are recovering from chemical dependence, they must begin to deal with things that they used to avoid by getting drunk or high. This includes stress. If group members used to get drunk or stoned when stressed out, how are they going to handle stress in positive ways now? We've got to teach them.

The activities in this section introduce a variety of approaches. The first set of activities will help group members identify their stressors, and what they now do when feeling stressed. And this section finishes with two popular techniques, deep muscle relaxation and positive imagery. Both of these have proven successful for relieving stress and will show group members there are other ways of coping with stress that don't involve getting drunk or high.

86
Coping with Stress

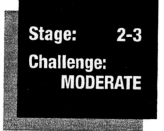

Stage: 2-3
Challenge: MODERATE

GOALS: ▶
- Evaluate personal stress level
- Learn variety of stress-reducing techniques

DESCRIPTION: ▶

Group members discuss a number of strategies for alleviating stress in their lives.

DIRECTIONS: ▶

Begin a discussion about stress—where it comes from and what happens to us when we're feeling it—by asking students to identify common stress-producing events, such as resisting peer pressure, going to a new school, or returning home from a chemical dependence treatment center. Then ask them to describe what happens when stress builds up in their bodies. Examples can include sleeplessness, headaches, irritability.

Using the blackboard, ask the group to make a list of different things they do when they are feeling stressed. At this point, don't judge the effectiveness of their strategies. Typical examples include running, staring at the wall, fighting, talking about the stress, screaming into a pillow. When they are finished offering examples, ask the group to decide which of the strategies are counterproductive—that is, strategies that either don't reduce the stress or may even increase it. For example, screaming at others when you're tense produces guilt and additional stress; staring at the wall and brooding is a passive response that does little to alleviate the problem. Erase those examples the group agrees are counterproductive.

For the remaining list, ask the person who mentioned the example to explain how he uses it in his life—under what circumstances and what the outcome is. When all the remaining examples have been discussed, ask group members to choose one strategy to use the next time they are feeling stressed. Discuss which strategies they chose and in what situations they will use it.

NOTES: ▶

If the group isn't able to produce very many different strategies for dealing with stress, be prepared to offer some for consideration. Here's a partial list: running, talking with a friend, screaming into a pillow, writing in a journal, limiting responsibilities, going to a twelve-step meeting, snoozing in the sun, playing sports, meditating, practicing relaxation, talking with your sponsor, deep breathing, daydreaming, reading a joke book, hanging out with friends.

MATERIALS: ▶

None required.

87
Where's the Stress in My Body?

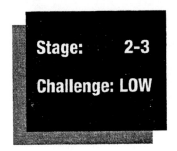

GOALS:

- Identify stressors
- Create awareness of personal reaction to stress
- Learn how to deal with stress

DESCRIPTION: ▶

Students draw outlines of their bodies and then locate and write descriptions of how stress feels to them.

DIRECTIONS: ▶

Begin a discussion about stress, focusing on how our physical bodies can react to stress. Students may describe stress manifested in their bodies as headaches, knotted stomachs, or pain in their lower back, for example.

Pass out large sheets of newsprint and ask group members to trace each other's outlines. When finished, ask them to write the different stressors they experience on the outside of their body outline, and then to describe the different ways in which their bodies respond to stress with arrows, pictures, and words. For example, a student might identify staying clean and sober, her father, dating, and starting a new class as stressors. And, also on the paper, she might draw an arrow to her forehead and describe the headaches she gets whenever she is feeling uptight about her father's drinking and arrows to her fists and describe how she always clenches her fists when she is nervous.

After everyone has finished, use the remaining time to discuss the drawings, asking group members to think of positive ways that help them deal with their stress.

QUESTIONS:

- How does stress feel to you?
- How can you tell when you are stressed?
- What situations are stressful for you?
- What do you do when you are stressed? Does this help?
- What else can you do to relieve your stress?
- What are common stress-related physical complaints and illnesses? Do you experience any of these?

MATERIALS:

Large sheets of newsprint, markers.

88
My Coping Style

Stage: 2-3
Challenge: MODERATE

GOALS: ▶
- Identify helpful coping strategies
- Identify student stressors that require new responses

DESCRIPTION: ▶
Students complete a worksheet that provides a focus for discussing how they deal with everyday pressures.

DIRECTIONS: ▶
Pass out copies of **My Coping Style** worksheet and ask students to complete it. When they are finished, ask a group member to read her coping response to the first item of the list. Ask the rest of the group if anyone else reacts similarly. Ask these students to stand together outside the group circle. Then ask one of the students remaining seated to share his response to the first pressure on the list. Again form a grouping of students who had a similar response. Continue this process until everyone is either in a small grouping or standing by themselves.

While everyone is still standing in subgroups, discuss the merits of their coping responses. Encourage debate between the subgroups. When finished, ask group members to return to their seats and begin this process again, using the second question on the worksheet.

QUESTIONS: ▶
(Direct these questions to the subgroups.)
- What is helpful about your coping response? What are the drawbacks?
- Does your response get rid of the stressful event?
- Which of the subgroups' coping responses is the most helpful?
- Which coping responses should you avoid using?

MATERIALS: ▶
My Coping Style worksheet.

My Coping Style

Consider your usual reactions when you answer the following questions.
When I'm:

1. Hearing my parents fight,	I cope by . . .
2. Feeling left out,	I cope by . . .
3. Feeling disappointed,	I cope by . . .
4. Feeling embarrassed,	I cope by . . .
5. Feeling angry,	I cope by . . .
6. Late for school,	I cope by . . .
7. Feeling lonely,	I cope by . . .
8. Being accused of something,	I cope by . . .
9. Fighting with my parents,	I cope by . . .
10. Feeling nervous and anxious,	I cope by . . .

89
Stress Reduction Through Relaxation

GOALS:

- Evaluate personal stress level
- Learn stress-reducing techniques

DESCRIPTION: ▶

Group members are taught a muscle relaxation exercise as a way to reduce stress in their lives.

DIRECTIONS: ▶

Introduce the concept of stress by asking group members for examples of stress-producing situations such as breaking up with a boyfriend, going to a new school, or parents fighting. Ask them to describe how stress feels and where it locates itself in their bodies, such as a tight stomach or a headache. Then ask them to describe what happens when stress builds up in their bodies (examples might include sleeplessness, stomachaches, irritability).

Tell the group you are going to teach them how they can relax their bodies by relaxing their muscles. Point out to them that they can't be relaxed and stressed at the same time, so if they can learn to relax when feeling stressed, the tension will disappear.

Ask everyone to find a comfortable spot on the floor to lie down. They should be flat on their backs, arms at their sides. Remind them that the purpose of this activity isn't to fall asleep but to experience deep relaxation. Now read in a slow, calm voice the **Muscle Relaxation Script** on the following page.

After the relaxation activity is finished, bring the group back together and ask them to discuss how this activity felt. Point out to the group that they can bring about this feeling of deep relaxation more and more quickly if they practice. Once they are proficient with this technique, they can relax their bodies and get rid of tension in many stressful situations, such as fighting the urge to get high or drunk, a speech in front of the class, or when things are tense at home.

Ask the group for suggestions as to when they could practice this activity (at night before falling asleep, or for ten minutes after school several times each week).

NOTES: ▶

This activity works best if your group room is carpeted; if not, bring pillows so the hard floor will be bearable. Chairs are the least desirable alternative.

MATERIALS: ▶

Muscle Relaxation Script.

Muscle Relaxation Script

"I am going to give you some instructions that will help you relax your muscles, starting with your arm muscles and ending with the muscles in your legs. For each set of muscles, I'm going to ask you to tighten them for a few seconds and then let them relax. As this happens your body will begin to feel more and more relaxed and your breathing will slow. Remember, though, the goal is to relax your body, not fall asleep. Let your mind wander and drift among peaceful thoughts and enjoy the activity. Let's begin.

"Make sure you're in a comfortable position. If you aren't, move around a bit. **(Wait for them to get adjusted.)** Now close your eyes and concentrate on your breathing. Take in a deep breath, deep until you feel your lungs stretch out. And now exhale. Again breathe in deep...and then exhale. Feel your heartbeat slowing and your body calming. Breathe in deep, deeper...and exhale. **(Pause for five seconds.)**

"Now I want you to imagine an orange in your right hand. Squeeze this hand tight... tight...tighter to get every last drop of juice...and now drop the orange out of your hand and let your hand fall limp at your side. Notice the difference between the tension and the relaxation. This is how many of the muscles feel in our body when we're stressed and uptight...and often without us even realizing it. Now pick up another orange with your right hand and squeeze it, tight...tight...tighter...and then drop the orange and notice your hand feels even more relaxed.

"Now let's work on your left hand. **(Repeat with the same instruction as for the right hand.)**

"Now you're going to stretch your arm and shoulder muscles by raising your arms up high behind your head. Join your hands together up behind your head and, while keeping them close to the floor, stretch them up behind your head like a cat stretching after an afternoon nap. Feel the tension in you arms and shoulders. Now hold that tight...tight...tighter...and then relax and bring your arms to your sides. Feel how relaxed and limp your arms are now. **(Pause a few seconds and repeat.)**

"Now let's focus on your neck muscles. Just like a turtle pulling its head into its shell, bring your head down into your shoulders, tight...tight...tighter...and now relax. **(Pause a few seconds and repeat.)**

"Now let's relax some of the muscles of your face. I want you to clench your jaw muscles by gritting your teeth together. Feel how tight your jaw muscles get when you do this? Clench them tight now...tight...tighter...and now relax and feel your jaw sag **(Pause a few seconds and then repeat.)**

"Oftentimes, our stomachs can get knotted up when we are feeling stress, so let's relax the muscles in the middle of our body. Imagine yourself about to be punched in the stomach and so you make your stomach muscles very tight. Hold it tight . . . tight . . . tighter . . . and now relax. Take a few slow deep breaths now, breathing in deep and then exhale . . . again breathe in . . . and exhale. Now tighten your stomach again . . . tight . . . tight . . . tighter . . . and now relax. Again concentrate on your breathing. You're feeling very relaxed now. Your body is heavy; your muscles loose and very relaxed. Your breathing very slow and steady.

"Now let's concentrate on your leg muscles. Starting with your right leg, I want you to tighten these muscles by stretching your leg out as far as it will go. Imagine that you are making yourself another foot taller because your leg is stretching out so far. Hold these muscles tight . . . tight . . . tighter . . . and now let them relax. **(Pause a few seconds and repeat.)**

continued on next page

MUSCLE RELAXATION SCRIPT CONTINUED . . .

"Now let's do the same thing with your left leg. Tighten your left thigh muscle tight . . . tight . . . tighter . . . and then relax **(Pause a few seconds and repeat.)**

Your feet also have lots of muscles that need relaxing. Clench the muscles of your right foot by imagining yourself picking up a softball by grabbing it with your toes. Hold your right foot muscles tight . . . tight . . . tighter . . . and now let them relax. **(Pause a few seconds and repeat.)**

"And now let's finish with your left foot. Pick up a softball with your toes and hold these muscles tight . . . tight . . . tighter . . . and then let them relax. **(Pause a few seconds and repeat.)**

"Now let's return to your breathing. Feel how slow and steady your chest rises and falls. Your body feels so heavy and your muscles so loose. Pure relaxation! Now I'll be quiet and give you a few minutes to enjoy this feeling. Let your mind drift and your breathing slow and I will speak again in a few minutes. **" (Give the group a few minutes to enjoy their relaxation.)**

90
Positive Imagery

GOALS: ▶
- Increase positive thinking patterns
- Reduce stressful feelings

DESCRIPTION: ▶
Group members are taught how to practice imagining positive thoughts about themselves and personal situations.

DIRECTIONS: ▶
Introduce the concept of critical and negative self-talk by listing some examples of how people are quick to put themselves down and judge themselves harshly. It would be especially helpful to give any personal examples of your own negative self-talk. Common examples include "I'll never get it right," "I'm not as attractive as she is," or "I'll probably mess up this speech I have to give in front of the class." Ask group members to share examples of their own negative thinking.

Tell the group that since these negative thoughts can affect both their feelings and behavior, you are going to teach them a method for thinking positive thoughts and imagining positive outcomes for situations in which they are involved.

First, ask group members to think of situations or common thought patterns in which they usually envision a negative outcome or are self-critical, such as worrying whether their friends like them, thinking that staying sober will always be a struggle for themselves, thinking that they're ugly. Then read the **Positive Imagery Script** on the following page.

After the positive imagery exercise, when everyone is back together in a circle, ask them to discuss their imaginary journeys.

Tell the group that they can use positive imagery whenever they are worrying about something or are giving themselves negative messages. All it takes is a minute or two to imagine a different, positive outcome.

QUESTIONS: ▶
- What was the negative situation you imagined?
- What was the positive outcome for your situation?
- How did that outcome feel?
- Was it difficult to imagine a positive ending?

MATERIALS: ▶
Positive Imagery Script.

Positive Imagery Script

First, they all need to find a spot, preferably on the floor, where they can be comfortable. Once everyone is settled, dim the lights and read the following script to them:

"I want you to close your eyes and move your body around a bit to make sure that you are settled and comfortable. Now breathe in deeply and slowly a few times. Each time you exhale, feel your body getting a little heavier and heavier. Imagine the tension in your body being exhaled right along with each breath. (Give them 20 seconds or so to relax.)

"Now that you are relaxed, I want you to imagine the situation that you are worried about. Place yourself back in this situation. Imagine your surroundings, any other people who are present, the colors, the sounds. Now instead of things going wrong, imagine a great finish to this situation—the best possible outcome. You're happy, everything works out, there's nothing left to worry about. Stay with these good feelings for a minute. (Give them a minute or so to do this task.)

"Now, I want you to come back to this group room. Listen to the sounds you hear in this room, go ahead and stretch a little if you want to. When you feel ready, open your eyes and join the group circle."

91
Good Times Without Chemicals

GOALS: ▶
- Expose students to a variety of alternative highs
- Encourage students to begin to have fun without chemicals

DESCRIPTION: ▶

Group members discuss ways to have fun without using chemicals and make a commitment to try one new activity that was discussed.

DIRECTIONS: ▶

Point out to the group that many young people who have been heavily involved with alcohol and other drugs don't know any other way of having a good time than to get high or drunk. Challenge the group to make a list on the blackboard of all the ways they can think of to have fun that don't involve chemicals. If necessary, also include guidelines that prohibit recreation that is harmful to self, other people, or property. When a group member gives an example, ask her to describe a time that she has participated in that form of recreation. For example, a group member might offer skiing as an example of something to do that doesn't involve chemicals; then she should describe a time that she went skiing and the fun she had. Besides the dramatic and exciting examples that the group will typically name, ask them to also think of examples that are easy to do, have no or little cost, and are readily available, such as going bike riding with a friend, seeing a movie, playing the guitar, kicking the hackie sack.

Once you have a comprehensive list on the board (don't hesitate to help out if they miss any obvious examples), ask group members to pick an example from the list they haven't experienced before that they would be willing and able to try during the next several weeks. Make sure the group understands you're asking them to make a commitment to do this activity, and that they should pick an activity that will be possible for them to try. Choose one of the following group sessions to discuss the results of their activities, so group members know when their deadline is for completing the activity they chose. During this follow-up session, ask group members to describe their activities and how they felt about it.

QUESTIONS: ▶
- Was this activity enjoyable? What did you like about it?
- Is this something that you will do again? Why or why not?
- What's different about recreation without chemicals as compared to recreation with chemicals?

MATERIALS: ▶

None required.

Section H:
Peer Pressure Activities

Recovering from chemical dependence requires teenagers to make a break from the crowd and strike out in a new direction. While this isn't easy for anyone, it's most difficult to accomplish during the teenage years, those years characterized by the all-importance of friends.

While peer pressure in some groups might involve getting straight As, or being on the starting team, for group members peer pressure translates into drinking or getting high. The ticket to be a member of their former crowd is to "party hearty." So, the classic struggle for recovering young people takes shape: lots of friends and social status versus sobriety and happiness.

Since group members are easily influenced by others, it's important that some group time is set aside to teach them ways to handle peer pressure or they won't stay sober very long. The activities in this section will help group members identify healthy and unhealthy friendships, how to respond to questions about why they don't get high anymore, as well as tutor them in refusal skills. It's these types of lessons that will equip them for the inevitability of "Hey, Jim, me and some other guys are going to go cruising around and drink a few beers tonight. Wanna come along?" If they're prepared, they'll be ready.

92
Qualities of a Good Friend

GOALS: ▶
- Identify the qualities of a good friend
- Encourage students to build healthy friendships

DESCRIPTION: ▶
Students discuss the qualities inherent to a good friend and assess their current friendships.

DIRECTIONS: ▶
Ask the group to make a list on the blackboard of the qualities a good friend should have, such as, "You can trust them," "They help you stay clean and sober," and "They make you feel good about yourself." When there's a comprehensive list, hand out copies of **My Friends** worksheet (see following page) to everyone. When they've completed the worksheet, spend the remaining time discussing their answers.

QUESTIONS: ▶
- How healthy are your friendships?
- How many of your friends don't use alcohol or other drugs?
- Do you spend most of your time with those friends who support your sobriety? If not, why?
- How could you improve your friendships?

NOTES: ▶
Some group members might not have many friends. This in itself is important information. Ask this person, "Why don't you have many friends?" "Do you wish you had more friends?" and "How does it feel not to have many friends?"

MATERIALS: ▶
My Friends worksheet.

My Friends

First list five friends below. Friend #1 should be the friend with whom you spend the most time and friend #5 should be the friend with whom you spend the least amount of time. Then write three positive qualities (she makes me laugh or he cares what happens to me, for example) and three negative qualities (she drinks too much or we only do what he wants to do, for example) for each friend listed.

Positive qualities	Friend's name	Negative qualities
1.	#1_____	1.
2.		2.
3.		3.
1.	#2_____	1.
2.		2.
3.		3.
1.	#3_____	1.
2.		2.
3.		3.
1.	#4_____	1.
2.		2.
3.		3.
1.	#5_____	1.
2.		2.
3.		3.

93
What Do I Tell My Friends?

Stage: 2-3
Challenge: MODERATE

GOALS: ▶
- Reduce shame and embarrassment
- Minimize isolating behaviors

DESCRIPTION: ▶

Group members discuss a variety of approaches for dealing with the issue of friends being aware of their chemical dependence.

DIRECTIONS: ▶

After introducing this topic, ask group members to give examples of when their chemical dependence and abstinence from chemicals has been an embarrassment. Typical examples include going to a party and someone asking why they aren't drinking, or coming back from treatment and other students asking them where they've been this past month.

After there are at least ten examples, go back over the list and ask the group to identify at least one positive solution for each problem listed. For example, the group might decide that the best thing to do is to use humor, such as, "I never drink when I'm sober," or to just be honest—"I was in a treatment program for a drinking problem."

NOTES: ▶

Be prepared to offer both typical problems to list on the board as well as possible solutions to these problems if the group gets stuck. As much as possible, though, keep the responsibility on the group's shoulders to think of solutions to the problems they identify.

MATERIALS: ▶

None required.

94
A Peer Pressure Continuum

GOALS:

- Identify different types of peer pressure
- Develop constructive solutions for resisting difficult peer pressure situations

DESCRIPTION: ▶

Students construct a continuum of personal peer pressure experiences and identify constructive solutions for each situation.

DIRECTIONS: ▶

Pass out the **Peer Pressure** worksheet (see following page) and ask group members to complete the first part (listing four situations in which peer pressure is a factor).

   After everyone has finished, go around the circle and ask group members to read their personal situations out loud. Typical examples will include being asked if you want to skip class and go get high, or being called weird because you won't snort the coke with everyone else. After hearing other examples, some group members might wish to change some of their own. Then they should complete the second part of the worksheet by listing constructive ways of dealing with this peer pressure. Tell group members that it's okay if they can't think of a way to deal with a specific instance of peer pressure. In that case, they should leave that number blank and go on to the next situation.

   When everyone is finished with the second part, ask them to describe how they could handle each of their four instances of peer pressure. Typical examples could include telling the person she can't because she's on the volleyball team, walking away, or talking about the situation with their sponsor. If someone was unable to think of a solution for a particular instance, ask the rest of the group for suggestions.

QUESTIONS:

- Will you be able to follow through with your solutions for dealing with peer pressure when you're asked to drink or get high?
- Are some methods of handling peer pressure better than others? Why?

MATERIALS:

Peer Pressure worksheet.

Peer Pressure

On the top half of the line, write four examples of situations when you've felt pressured by your peers to use alcohol or other drugs. Example #1 should be an example that was very easy to deal with; example #4 should be the most difficult instance of peer pressure you've experienced.

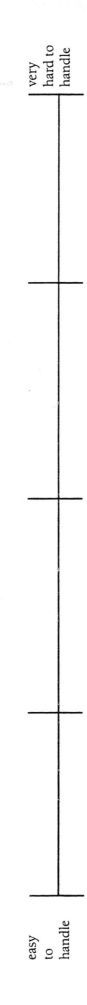

easy to handle

very hard to handle

Now on the bottom half of this line, write how you could resist the peer pressure in each example up above the line.

95
Self-assertion
Role Plays

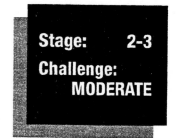

GOALS:

- Teach students the difference between passive, assertive, and aggressive behavior
- Practice appropriate responses in realistic settings

DESCRIPTION: ▶

Students examine the differences between passive, assertive, and aggressive responses and practice appropriate responses using role plays.

DIRECTIONS: ▶

Begin this session by asking group members to explain the difference between passive, assertive, and aggressive responses to problem situations. Once they understand these differences, ask group members to describe their typical manner of responding to problems involving other people, such as a friend who keeps forgetting to repay borrowed money. Through this discussion, it will become apparent that a group member's response style depends on the situation and whether the other person is a friend, parent, or stranger.

　　Pass out the **Passive, Assertive, and Aggressive Responses** worksheet on the following page. After they have completed it, ask a group member to pick one of the situations on the worksheet and role-play her assertive response, using other group members to stand in for other necessary roles. After she has finished the role play, ask the rest of the group to comment on her response using the questions below as a guideline. When the discussion is finished, ask her to choose another group member to continue the activity with his choice of role plays.

QUESTIONS:

- Was the response passive, assertive, or aggressive?
- Are there other responses that would work as well?
- Have any of you been in this situation before? How did you respond?
- How does it feel when you respond passively to a problem? Assertively? Aggressively?

MATERIALS:

Passive, Assertive, and Aggressive Responses worksheet.

Passive, Assertive, and Aggressive Responses

For each of the situations below, write three different types of responses that would be typical for you.

SITUATION #1:
Your English teacher seems to have always had it in for you. Now that you're back from treatment and staying clean and sober, he still seems to pick on you, even though you're trying hard to do well in his class. Today, you and several other students were one minute late for his class and he started yelling at you.

A passive response:
An aggressive response:
An assertive response:

SITUATION #2:
A friend borrowed some lunch money, promising to pay you back the next day. Two weeks have gone by and he always has a new excuse. It's not a lot of money but you are feeling used and angry.

A passive response:
An aggressive response:
An assertive response:

SITUATION #3:
Your boyfriend, Tim, gets jealous easily. A friend of yours, who happens to be a guy, sits with you occasionally during lunch. Today, Tim came into the lunchroom and saw the two of you together. He came over and pulled you aside, demanding you don't sit with this guy.

A passive response:
An aggressive response:
An assertive response:

SITUATION #4:
Describe a problem situation you sometimes experience.

A passive response:
An aggressive response:
An assertive response:

96
Learning How to Say "No"

GOALS:

- Identify a variety of ways to resist peer pressure to use mind-altering chemicals
- Practice using these new skills

DESCRIPTION: ▶

Students identify, through group discussion and with help from the group leader, techniques for resisting peer pressure to use alcohol or other drugs. These new skills are practiced through role playing.

DIRECTIONS:

After introducing the topic, ask students to list different methods for resisting peer pressure to use alcohol or other drugs. Ask a group member to record these examples on the chalkboard. The examples can be both strategies the students have used before or ones they think would work. Typical examples include saying, "No thanks, I don't feel like it," walking away from the person offering the beer or joint, or saying, "Naw, they mess me up too much." If the group is having difficulties providing examples, you might want to ask them to think of a particular situation first and then think of the response. Ask them how they would handle someone offering them a joint out in the school parking lot, or at a party, for example.

Once they've listed a number of methods on the board, the group should choose one to role play. Ask for volunteers for the variety of parts: one student to say no, a student to offer the beer or joint, several others to play supporting roles such as other people at the party, and friends of either of the first two students.

Once the roles are assigned, give the group members a few minutes to create a short role play. You might want to tell them to go over into the corner of the room, away from the rest of the group, to work out the details. When they are ready, they should act out the scenario for the rest of the group.

When they have finished the role play, discuss the scenario with the group. Has anyone in group been in this type of situation before? Was it difficult or easy to handle? What are some other responses that could be used in this situation?

Depending on the remaining time, act out new situations from the list on the blackboard with different group members.

NOTES: ▶

If your support group members are having a tough time getting into character, you could help out by playing a role, too. Or you may want to select group members who are natural clowns for the initial role play. You might also want to provide props to make the scene realistic: an empty beer can, taped party music, a steering wheel.

MATERIALS:

Theatrical props, if desired.

Section I: Group Challenge Activities

Recovering young people discover right away that if they're going to stay clean and sober, it's going to happen with the help of other people—an addict alone is in bad company, as a slogan from N.A. points out.

Yet reaching out to others isn't always easy. A macho, make-it-on-your-own attitude, fear of rejection, or a personality style that is isolating and closed can hinder these teenagers from experiencing the power and serenity of community with others. That's what makes a support group so important for these young people. We give them a regular time to connect with their peers who are experiencing similar struggles.

But besides giving them time and a place to connect, we can encourage them to nurture and expand these connections with their peers. The strengthening of these bonds, like a muscle, happens with exercise and challenge.

The activities in this section will encourage them to plan and work together towards goals that *the group* identifies as important. This not only builds a sense of community, it encourages group members to decide what's important for themselves and to take the responsibility for the follow-through. In doing so, these young people have come full circle—from the powerlessness of addiction to the power of taking care of themselves.

97
Ask the Question

Stage: 3

Challenge: HIGH

GOALS: ▶
- Encourage discussion of important and relevant issues
- Increase the trust level of the group

DESCRIPTION: ▶

Group members take turns asking each other questions relevant to the group experience.

DIRECTIONS: ▶

Explain to the group that the purpose of this activity is to find out more about each other and to encourage discussion of issues that are important but sometimes difficult to talk about. Begin by asking the first question directed to a single group member. The person who answers your question creates the next question and decides whom she would like to answer it. If the person being asked the question doesn't wish to answer, he can simply say "pass." In this case, the person asking the question can then choose a new group member.

NOTES: ▶

As long as the questions don't get too ridiculous or unproductive, resist the temptation to jump in and take charge. Group members need to work this out on their own.

MATERIALS: ▶

None required.

98
The Student Takeover

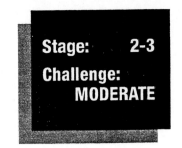

Stage: 2-3
Challenge: MODERATE

GOALS: ▶

- Encourage students to take responsibility for their group
- Encourage students to think about their needs

DESCRIPTION: ▶

Group members are given the opportunity to plan and then facilitate the following week's group session.

DIRECTIONS: ▶

Inform the group that during the next week of group they are to be in charge. This means deciding what the focus should be, what activity they should use, how they will divide responsibilities, and what materials they need. Help them plan the group session by addressing these questions in a constructive order.

First off, they need to decide what is an important group topic for them by discussing what it is that they need. Typical examples might include talking more about their feelings, learning how to handle anger, or discussing specific problems related to staying clean and sober.

Next, they should find an activity that focuses on this topic. They might want to invent their own activity (this should be encouraged), or you could show them this book as well as suggest other ideas. The final step is to decide how to divide the responsibilities for the group activity. The following week of group should be reserved for them to follow through with their plan.

NOTES: ▶

Even though they might be disorganized, resist the temptation to jump in and rescue the group. They'll work it out. And after all, though it might not run smoothly, it's their plan.

MATERIALS: ▶

Activity ideas, if they request them.

99
Group Graffiti

GOALS: ▶
- ■ Encourage free expression of thoughts and feelings
- ■ Create group unity

DESCRIPTION: ▶
A large sheet of newsprint is taped to the group room wall for students to draw artwork or express thoughts and feelings.

DIRECTIONS: ▶
Using bulletin board paper or large sheets of newsprint, cover a large area of a wall in the group room. Tell the group that they can write and draw whatever they wish as long as it relates to their thoughts and feelings in connection with the group experience. Leave the mural on the wall until the final session of group so that each session they can continue to add to the mural.

NOTES: ▶
If you have different groups that meet in the same room, either use different walls for each or take the murals down after each session. Also keep an eye out for negative or hurtful put-downs that a group member might write on the mural.

Depending on the other uses of your group room and the types of walls, you may wish to allow the group to use a small portion of the actual wall to decorate as a group project. Over the course of many groups and years, the group room wall can become a beautiful patchwork quilt of many different group members and group experiences.

MATERIALS: ▶
Poster paper or newsprint and markers.

100
Group Video

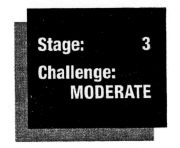
GOALS: ▶
- Increase awareness of the effects of chemical dependence
- Provide opportunities for group members to express their concerns and frustrations

DESCRIPTION: ▶

Group members make a short video dramatizing what it's like to be recovering from chemical dependence.

DIRECTIONS: ▶

The first step is to write a script. One student should record the ideas as the rest of the group discusses possibilities for the video script. It will be helpful first to choose a focused, specific topic such as how to stay clean and sober, or what school-based support groups are all about.

After the script is written, character roles should be assigned to the group members and the script rehearsed until students are comfortable with their parts. The video can then be taped by either a group member or group leader.

Group members can share their personal experiences during the writing phase of this project, but they shouldn't act out their own roles; it's easier and emotionally safer to act out roles other than their own. This policy also protects students' confidentiality.

NOTES: ▶

This isn't an activity to use in a support group with time constraints. Typically, you should allow for three group sessions to complete this project.

Also keep in mind that the main purpose of this activity is to provide a constructive outlet for students to express their concerns, not to make a slick, professional video. The process, not the product, is what's important.

MATERIALS: ▶

Video equipment such as a camera, tripod, tapes, VCR, and monitor.

101
The Great Escape

GOALS:
- Show students different ways to have fun
- Provide a reward for work done in group

DESCRIPTION:

Students plan an enjoyable activity that takes them out of the school building as a future reward they can work towards in the group.

DIRECTIONS:

Many chemically dependent adolescents remark that they used alcohol and other drugs because their lives are so boring. Often they think that sobriety will really be boring. Challenge the group to think of something that would be lots of fun that they can do together as a group, such as going to a park and having a picnic, going skiing, canoeing, to an amusement park, or on a hike.

Since this activity will most likely require school cooperation in terms of money, time and staff, ask the group what they are willing to do in exchange. Perhaps the challenge might be requiring everyone to be clean and sober for the remainder of the semester (with the activity at the end of the semester), or that everyone attend at least six 12-step meetings.

Involve group members in the planning as much as possible. This is their event. Decide what steps need to be taken, how the group will know whether everyone met the challenge, what to do if someone fails the challenge, when the activity will be, how much it will cost. Once all the planning is done, monitor the challenge at the beginning of each group session—"Did everyone remain abstinent from all chemicals this week?" for example.

NOTES:

Before introducing this activity, check out your ideas with your building principal. It would be a shame to get the students all worked up and then have to come back the following session and tell them that they can't do it.

Don't hesitate to ask for help from other adults in your school or community. You needn't take this project on all by yourself.

MATERIALS:

None required for the planning stage.

Appendix A: Feelings List

afraid	guilty	threatened	powerful
envious	jealous	comfortable	unneeded
respected	bitter	horrified	disappointed
aggressive	happy	miserable	irritated
exasperated	joyful	thrilled	anxious
sad	surprised	concerned	glad
alarmed	bored	hostile	shocked
excited	helpless	needed	powerless
safe	lonely	troubled	unsure
amused	tense	confident	discouraged
frightened	calm	hurt	puzzled
satisfied	hopeful	nervous	wanted
angry	loved	uneasy	eager
frustrated	terrified	confused	regretful
scared	afraid	inadequate	worried
annoyed	envious	paranoid	rejected
furious	respected	unimportant	worthless
secure	aggressive	contented	enraged
anxious	exasperated	perplexed	relieved
glad	sad	unloved	worthwhile
shocked	hopeless	crushed	enthusiastic
appreciated	mad	insecure	resentful

Appendix B:
The Twelve Steps

1. We admitted we were powerless over alcohol—that our lives had become unmanageable.

2. Came to believe that a Power greater than ourselves could restore us to sanity.

3. Made a decision to turn our will and our lives over to the care of God *as we understood Him*.

4. Made a searching and fearless moral inventory of ourselves.

5. Admitted to God, to ourselves, and to another human being the exact nature of our wrongs.

6. We were entirely ready to have God remove all these defects of character.

7. Humbly asked Him to remove our shortcomings.

8. Made a list of all persons we had harmed, and became willing to make amends to them all.

9. Made direct amends to such people whenever possible, except when to do so would injure them or others.

10. Continued to take personal inventory and when we were wrong promptly admitted it.

11. Sought through prayer and meditation to improve our conscious contact with God *as we understood Him*, praying only for knowledge of his will for us and the power to carry that out.

12. Having had a spiritual awakening as a result of these steps, we tried to carry this message to alcoholics, and to practice these principles in all our affairs.

Resources

NOTE: ▶

Most of the following materials are available from Hazelden Publishing and Educational Services. Please call us at 1-800-328-9000, or visit our website at www.hazelden.org.

BOOKS: ▶

A.A. World Services. *Twelve Steps and Twelve Traditions.*

Anderson, Gary L. *When Chemicals Come to School: The Student Assistance Model.*

Fleming, Martin. *Conducting Support Groups for Students Affected by Chemical Dependence: A Guide for Educators and Other Professionals.*

Fleming, Martin. *101 Support Group Activities for Teenagers Affected by Someone Else's Alcohol/Drug Use.*

Fleming, Martin. *101 Support Group Activities for Teenagers at Risk for Chemical Dependence or Related Problems.*

Freeman, Shelley MacKay. *From Peer Pressure to Peer Support: Alcohol and Other Drug Prevention Through Group Process—A Curriculum for Grades 7-12.*

Jesse, Rosalie Cruise. *Children in Recovery.*

Johnson, Vernon. *Intervention: How to Help Someone Who Doesn't Want Help.*

Leite, Evelyn, and Pamela Espeland. *Different Like Me: A Book for Teens Who Worry About Their Parents' Use of Alcohol/Drugs.*

Schaefer, Dick. *Choices and Consequences: What to Do When a Teenager Uses Alcohol/Drugs.*

Schmidt, Teresa, and Thelma Spencer. *Building Trust, Making Friends: Tanya Talks About Chemical Dependence in the Family (grades 6-8)*

BOOKLETS: ▶

Cloninger, Robert. *Genetic and Environmental Factors Leading to Alcoholism.*

Daley, Dennis & Judy Miller. *Recovery and Relapse Prevention for Parents of Chemically Dependent Children.*

Daley, Dennis & Judy Miller. *When Your Child Is Chemically Dependent.*

Leite, Evelyn. *Detachment: The Art of Letting Go While Living with an Alcoholic.*

Leite, Evelyn. *How It Feels to Be Chemically Dependent.*

WORKBOOKS: ▶

Fleming, Martin. *How to Stay Clean and Sober: A Relapse Prevention Guide for Teenagers.*

Sassatelli, Jean. *Breaking Away: Saying Goodbye to Alcohol/Drugs.*

Zarek, David and James Sipe. *Can I Handle Alcohol/Drugs?*

PERIODICALS:

Focus on the Family and Chemical Dependence. 2119-A Hollywood Blvd., Hollywood, FL 33020.

Student Assistance Journal. 1863 Technology Drive, Troy, MI 48083.

VIDEOS:

All the Kids Do It. Color, 35 minutes. Pyramid, 1537 14th Street, Box 1048, Santa Monica, CA 90406.

Another Chance to Change. Color, 30 minutes. Johnson Institute.

Bridging the Gap. Color, 22 minutes. Sterling Productions, Inc. 500 N. Dearborn Street, #119, Chicago, IL 60610.

Choices and Consequences. Color, 33 minutes. Johnson Institute.

Different Like Me: For Teenage Children of Alcoholics. Color, 31 minutes. Johnson Institute.

My Father's Son: The Legacy of Alcoholism. Color, 33 minutes. Gerald T. Rogers Productions, 5225 Old Orchard Road, Suite 23A, Skokie, IL 60077.

Soft Is the Heart of A Child. Color, 30 minutes. Operation Cork, 8939 Villa La Jolla Drive, San Diego, CA 92037.

A Story About Feelings. Color, 10 minutes. Johnson Institute.

Tell Someone: A Music Video. Color, 4 minutes. Addiction Counselors Continuing Education Services, P.O. Box 30380, Indianapolis, IN 46230.

Where's Shelley? Color, 13 minutes. Johnson Institute.

Wasted: A True Story. Color, 28 minutes. MTI Teleprograms, Inc. 3710 Commercial Avenue, Northbrook, IL 60062.

OTHER MATERIALS:

Black, Claudia. *The Stamp Game.* MAC Publishing 5005 E. 39th Avenue, Denver, CO 80207, (303) 331-0148.

NATIONAL ORGANIZATIONS:

Children of Alcoholics Foundation, Inc. (COAF)
P.O. Box 4185
Grand Central Station
New York, NY 10163
(212) 754-0656

Johnson Institute
7205 Ohms Lane
Minneapolis, MN 55439-2159
(612) 831-1630 or (800) 231-5165

National Association for Children of Alcoholics (NACoA)
11426 Rockville Pike, Suite 100
Rockville, MD 20852
(301) 468-0985

National Council on Alcoholism and Drug Dependence (NCADD)
12 West 21st Street
New York, NY 10010
(212) 206-6770